SUCCEEDING WITH
INQUIRY
IN
SCIENCE AND MATH
CLASSROOMS

Founded in 1943, ASCD provides expert and innovative solutions in professional development, capacity building, and educational leadership essential to the way educators learn, teach, and lead. ASCD's 140,000 members include superintendents, principals, teachers, professors, and advocates from more than 134 countries. www.ascd.org

The National Science Teachers Association (NSTA), founded in 1944 and headquartered in Arlington, Virginia, is the largest organization in the world committed to promoting excellence and innovation in science teaching and learning for all. NSTA's current membership of 60,000 includes science teachers, science supervisors, administrators, scientists, business and industry representatives, and others involved in and committed to science education. www.nsta.org

SUCCEEDING WITH INQUIRY
IN
SCIENCE AND MATH
CLASSROOMS

JEFF C. MARSHALL

ASCD
Alexandria, Virginia USA

NSTApress
Arlington, Virginia USA

1703 N. Beauregard St. • Alexandria, VA 22311-1714 USA
Phone: 800-933-2723 or 703-578-9600 • Fax: 703-575-5400
Website: www.ascd.org • E-mail: member@ascd.org
Author guidelines: www.ascd.org/write

1840 Wilson Blvd. • Arlington, VA 22201 USA
Phone: 703-243-7100 • Fax: 703-243-7177
Customer service: 800-277-5300
Website: www.nsta.org/store • E-mail: nstapress@nsta.org

Published simultaneously by ASCD, 1703 N. Beauregard Street, Alexandria, VA 22311 (www.ascd.org) and National Science Teachers Association, 1840 Wilson Blvd., Arlington, VA 22201 (www.nsta.org).

ASCD Staff: Gene R. Carter, *Executive Director;* Mary Catherine (MC) Desrosiers, *Chief Program Development Officer;* Richard Papale, *Publisher;* Laura Lawson, *Acquisitions Editor;* Julie Houtz, *Director, Book Editing & Production;* Darcie Russell, *Editor;* Thomas Lytle, *Graphic Designer;* Mike Kalyan, *Production Manager;* Valerie Younkin, *Desktop Publishing Specialist,* Andrea Wilson, *Production Specialist*

Printed in the United States of America. Cover art © 2013 by ASCD. ASCD publications present a variety of viewpoints. The views expressed or implied in this book should not be interpreted as official positions of the Association.

All referenced trademarks are the property of their respective owners.

Material in Chapter 7 was drawn from Marshall, J. C., & Horton, R. M. (2009). Developing, assessing, and sustaining inquiry-based instruction: A guide for math and science teachers and leaders. Saarbruecken, Germany: VDM Publishing House Ltd., Chapter 6: Managing an inquiry effectively, pp. 87–112. Used by permission.

EQUIP is based upon the work by the National Science Foundation under Grant #DRL-0952160 and by the South Carolina Center of Excellence in Inquiry in Mathematics and Science Grant funded by the Commission on Higher Education.

All web links in this book are correct as of the publication date below but may have become inactive or otherwise modified since that time. If you notice a deactivated or changed link, please e-mail books@ascd.org with the words "Link Update" in the subject line. In your message, please specify the web link, the book title, and the page number on which the link appears.

PAPERBACK ISBN: 978-1-4166-1608-5

ASCD product #113008   n10/13

Also available as an e-book (see Books in Print for the ISBNs)

Quantity discounts: 10–49 copies, 10%; 50+ copies, 15%; for 1,000 or more copies, call 800-933-2723, ext. 5634, or 703-575-5634. For desk copies: www.ascd.org/deskcopy

Library of Congress Cataloging-in-Publication Data
Marshall, Jeff C., 1965–
 Succeeding with inquiry in science and math classrooms / Jeff C. Marshall.
   pages cm
Includes bibliographical references and index.
 ISBN 978-1-4166-1608-5 (pbk. : alk. paper) 1. Inquiry-based learning. 2. Classroom management. 3. Science—Study and teaching. 4. Mathematics—Study and teaching. I. Title.
LB1027.23.M28 2008
371.39—dc23

                                                                                    2013025542

22 21 20 19 18 17 16 15 14 13   1 2 3 4 5 6 7 8 9 10 11 12

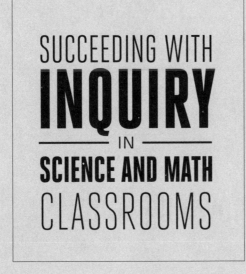

SUCCEEDING WITH
INQUIRY
— IN —
SCIENCE AND MATH
CLASSROOMS

Acknowledgments

I am very fortunate to know and work with many great teachers and scholars who inspire me to continue to learn and grow. My ongoing fascination with science and learning has been present since I was in grade school. Today my greatest learning comes from watching my own children, Anna and Ben, grow and develop; their curiosity about how the world works is always fun to witness. My college students also continue to invigorate my thirst to know and understand the complex world of teaching and learning.

It is with great appreciation that I acknowledge the contributions of Robert Horton, a math educator from Clemson University. Our partnership over the last six years has helped me better understand the complexities of transforming instructional practice in math education. He has been instrumental in co-developing Chapters 4 and 5, which describe specific applications of inquiry in science and math settings. We hope our ideas affirm the critical importance that inquiry-based instruction plays in deep, meaningful K–20 science and mathematics education.

Finally, my research and writing on teacher transformation in science and mathematics classrooms has been successful in part because of the support received from two major grants. This material is based on the work supported by the National Science Foundation under Grant #DRL-0952160 and a grant from the South Carolina Commission on Higher Education under the auspices of the EIA Teacher Education Centers of Excellence Grant Program. Any opinions, findings, conclusions, or recommendations expressed in this material are those of the author and do not necessarily reflect the views of the National Science Foundation.

Introduction

While reading a book or listening to a presentation on teaching practices, do you ever catch yourself thinking, "Yeah, I already know that"? Well, this book will help you progress beyond that sort of passive acknowledgment to a deeper exploration of your teaching and, specifically, the beliefs that inform it, the practices that guide it, and the actions that facilitate it. For administrators and instructional coaches, your active involvement is just as critical.

You are likely to take either of two general approaches as you read this book, each with dramatically different outcomes. You can be actively involved by continually asking how an idea or topic relates to your practice, students, department, school, and district. Or you can scan the book, grabbing a few tips to try out in tomorrow's lesson. The first approach seeks to transform your teaching practice by improving its overall quality over time; the second approach, though common, aims for a few modest tweaks, often neglecting any long-term improvements.

TIP

To encourage thought and discussion, I've included notes called Transformations in Practice (TIPs) throughout the book. When you come to each tip, I hope you will pause and explicitly reflect on your practice, instruction, or perceptions related to the immediate topic.

Chapter 1 begins by helping you examine your current values, practices, and actions as teachers. It helps you to understand the unique perspectives and approaches that you bring to the classroom. In so doing, you can target areas that need improvement as well as those where you excel.

The remaining chapters will address the details needed to make such instruction successful. Chapter 2 makes the case for why inquiry should be a critical component of instruction and learning when the major ideas are tackled in your discipline or at your grade level. If you are an advocate of inquiry-based instruction, then your goal becomes how to improve the quality of the inquiry in your classroom.

Knowing and even valuing the importance of inquiry-based instruction does not mean inquiry automatically plays a leading role in your classroom. Chapter 3 assists with transforming your instruction by providing a framework that unites three major learning constructs that have been shown to improve student achievement: inquiry instruction, formative assessment, and reflective practice.

After years of hearing about the importance of inquiry-based instruction from commission reports, state and national standards, and leaders in education, many educators are at the point of understanding the basics of inquiry. However, most do not know *explicitly* how to plan and implement high-quality inquiry-based instruction. Chapters 4 and 5 discuss what inquiry looks like in science and mathematics classrooms. Chapter 4 discusses short examples for a wide range of core concepts, and Chapter 5 models inquiry-based instruction for a science unit and a mathematics unit.

Success with your lessons is ultimately not based on the curriculum or even the instruction but on the level of success your students experience. While end-of-unit and annual assessments help you understand how meaningful your students' learning was, you can tap some predictors for success well before then. Chapter 6 explores 19 things that teachers can do that are directly correlated with student achievement in science and mathematics. Using these predictive indicators, you can project how students will do on both content knowledge and process skill assessments based on teacher performance.

During nearly two decades of teaching both students and teachers, I have realized that motivation, desire, and knowledge are critical to leading inquiry-based instruction. However, without proper classroom management, lessons can quickly unravel, and you may be tempted to throw up your hands and say, "Inquiry is just not possible with my students." Chapter 7 looks at effectively managing an inquiry-focused classroom. With key findings from brain research and educational psychology, you will learn how to remove or significantly reduce the barriers that may try to block your students from successful inquiry-based learning.

Finally, Chapter 8 summarizes how inquiry-based instruction can become a cornerstone of your teaching. This chapter will help you to develop an individual plan for success and serve as a guide to transform your classroom.

1

Need for
INQUIRY
in Your Classroom

1

What Are Your Values, Practices, and Actions as a Teacher?

Should you just roll the dice, or is there a better way to determine the instructional strategies and assessments used to guide today's lesson? You are rolling the dice if you choose an instructional strategy based on what is easiest, what you haven't used in a while, or what your default strategy is. This lack of intentionality in your approach assumes that there is not a best—or at least not a better—way to instruct. It is a crapshoot because some days it works, but perhaps not for every student that day or for the whole class when your students are tested on the material.

Just as all our students come with unique experiences and backgrounds, we as teachers all have different experiences and training that prepare us to excel or flounder in the classroom. In this chapter, you will examine the experiences, beliefs, values, and actions that frame your daily teaching practice. An honest self-assessment will provide a starting point from which you can develop clear targeted objectives. Each objective comes with examples of what it looks like and what you need to do to move toward more effective instructional practice.

The difference in student achievement in a classroom led by an exemplary teacher is about 12 months greater than that of the student achievement led by a poorly performing teacher. Specifically, the students in the classroom of exemplary teachers on average progress the equivalent of 18 months in a single academic year versus 6 months of growth for students in the classroom of poorly performing teachers (Rice, 2003). The greatest academic growth is not dependent upon students' gender, race, or socio-economic status. Rather, the teacher's effectiveness is the single greatest determinant of student success (Darling-Hammond, 2000).

Our students deserve at least 12 months of growth each year from each teacher, and inquiry-based instruction can help you achieve that feat. Furthermore, research shows that students of teachers who have been part of our professional development and have been encouraged to use more and better inquiry-based instruction tend to outperform a similarly matched control group of students by two to seven months of academic growth (Marshall, 2012).

The common theme of various components of this chapter, whether flying at 30,000 feet or zooming in at ground level, is the importance of being an intentional practitioner. We are all intentional at some level, but how well we target our planning, instruction, interactions, and vision toward truly improving the achievement of all students is the subject of this book. Specifically, we will focus on succeeding with students in inquiry-based learning environments. Figure 1.1 gives an overview of values, practices, and actions that we explore in this chapter.

Figure 1.1
Perspectives That Inform Your Values and Practices

Perspective	Core Values and Practices	Question to Address
30,000′	Teaching philosophy	What do you value?
10,000′	Core ideas	What is truly important for students to know and be able to do?
1,000′	Success	How do you know when students have been successful?
100′	Strategies	How are students engaged in learning?
Ground level	Interactions, relationships, and learning	How can learning be maximized?

What Do You Value?

Your teaching philosophy provides the broad 30,000-foot (global) perspective of what you value as a teacher. Let's explore your philosophy.

TIP Your Values

Take a moment to write your teaching philosophy in one to two concise sentences—your elevator presentation of what you value as a teacher. You may need several drafts before you meaningfully capture who you are as a science or math educator. Remember, your philosophy statement is a dynamic statement and should evolve as you grow as an educator over the years.

If you are like most readers, you might now begin to peek ahead to see what the "right" answer is. After all, our educational upbringing has taught us to look for the single right answer instead of seeking thoughtful, unique solutions—a challenge that I address in this book.

It may seem counterproductive at this point to state your teaching philosophy, but I assure you that you will be continually referring to it as you read this book. As you form your philosophy, consider some of the following issues: What is your belief about student success in your class? What fosters student success in your class? What is your role in such success? What do students experience in your classroom that maximizes learning? In our quick-paced, sound-bite, hurry-on-to-the-next-fad world, you may be inclined to skip this exercise, but the explicit reflection on and acknowledgment of your beliefs, values, and actions is critical for moving your practice forward.

What Is Truly Important?

The next level of actions and values to consider, perhaps the 10,000-foot view, describes what core ideas (major concepts) students should know and be able to do when they complete your class. Core ideas are defined in a myriad of ways, but here they refer to the essential ideas or the 8 to 10 things that you want your students to know or be able to do by the end of the year. These core ideas are guided by district, state, or national standards and essentially compose the foundation of your curriculum, instruction, assessment, and classroom discourse, but they can be useful in other ways. You can provide core ideas to parents, students, and administrators as they seek to better understand the major instructional goals of your class, which when concisely stated in layman's terms allows all stakeholders to better support you and your program.

Interestingly, award-winning teachers view standards differently from most experienced mathematics and science teachers (Hudson, McMahon, & Overstreet, 2002; Marshall, 2008). Specifically, award-winning teachers tend to view national standards (National Council of Teachers of Mathematics [NCTM], 2000; National Research Council, 1996) as a framework to guide their classroom instruction, whereas other math and science teachers with 10 years of experience or more tend to view the standards as an obstacle that needs to be overcome or a collection of items that need to be "covered." With the 2013 Next Generation Science Standards (NGSS) and the 2010 Common Core State Standards in Mathematics (CCSSM), this tendency will continue—exemplary teachers will see standards as a guide for instruction whereas other will see standards as obstacles—unless something changes.

In science, a core idea for a chemistry class might include "Students will understand the trends and interactions found on the Periodic Table of Elements." This core idea requires that students demonstrate understanding of things such as periodic trends, reactivity of elements and relative strengths, and the way chemical formulas are written based on characteristics of various elements. In mathematics, core ideas may include "Algebra I students will develop an understanding of statistical variability for 6th-grade students" and "Students will represent and solve equations and inequalities graphically."

 TIP Core Ideas

What are the 8 to 10 core ideas that you want your students to really understand by the end of the school year? Why are these the most critical ideas? What are the least essential topics, ideas, or lessons that you currently teach? How can you trim or minimize the time that these lower-priority items consume in your class, and how will you use this additional time better?

When Have Your Students Been Successful?

For many teachers, teaching is about planning a lesson, implementing that lesson, and then checking to see how well students understand the material. On the surface, this approach sounds fine, but it typically leads to surface-level, fact-based learning that emphasizes memorization over thinking and recall over active engagement. So, at this 1,000-foot view, let's look a little deeper into the cycle that we commonly use (plan, implement, and assess).

First, the typical teacher realizes that there are standards that must be taught, so she seeks a lesson or activity from the resource guide or Internet that covers the topic mentioned in the standard. Then, if lucky, the teacher finds a quiz or assessment that goes along with the activity to measure student knowledge. The grade, for this one of the five (you fill in the number) required quizzes for the quarter, implies how well each student knows and understands that particular standard.

Let's contrast this approach with another one. First, the teacher clearly identifies and acknowledges what core idea frames the learning. Within that core idea, she articulates the major concepts that students will master by the end of the unit. Next, she determines how she will know when students have been successful and to what degree. Notice that determining how student mastery will be assessed precedes and guides the instruction to be developed—not the other way around. Then the teacher develops an instructional sequence that helps lead students toward mastery.

In the first approach, the teacher assumes that the assessment found with the lesson or activity is purposeful and appropriate for measuring student achievement relative to a given standard. That may be the case, but this approach still leaves the assessment in someone else's hands to determine what is valued and whether the learning measured will be lower-level, higher-level, or somewhere in between. The second approach uses the core idea to frame the learning, and the assessment is crafted to measure the degree of mastery of the concepts surrounding that big idea. Keep in mind that assessments created by other sources are not always inappropriate. Rather, it simply means that when we use assessments from other sources, we need to be intentional about what we use and why we are using all or part of it. We can quantify anything in order to create a grade to post, but the grade needs to be more than a number or letter. It needs to reflect student knowledge and/or degree of mastery relative to the concepts being studied or at least as close as possible.

To further illustrate the point, let's consider student performance in two different science classrooms. Teacher A gives a 10-question multiple-choice quiz that contains only recall or vocabulary-related items, and Teacher B gives a 10-question quiz that contains 4 recall-type questions, 4 application questions, and 2 higher-order questions. After they grade the quizzes, Teacher A and Teacher B both have the same class average—84 percent. When the grades go home, students in both classes seem to be performing equally well as a whole, when in fact the knowledge assessed in Teacher B's class is much deeper. Teacher A measured student success in defining vocabulary, whereas Teacher B measured student success in understanding, applying, and possibly doing science. The point is the same whether in science or in mathematics: we need to make sure that we are rigorously measuring and guiding student success relative to scientific and mathematical thinking. Measuring the success of instruction and learning will be central to Chapter 6.

How Are Students Involved?

We have progressed from what you value (educational philosophy statement) to the major concepts that students must know and be able to do (the core ideas), to how we know when students have been successful. Now we zoom in to consider the actions or strategies that you use to guide learning. Notice this sequence may seem backward—curriculum and instruction work often begins with a topic (the next section in your textbook) or activity (something that looks fun and engaging to students) and then progresses to finding the standard that it addresses.

Instead, this book will help you become intentional about the strategies you use to maximize learning. Although no two days will be exactly alike in terms of instruction, think about what your students typically experience. Begin by drawing two pie charts. The first chart should be titled General Classroom Organization and requires you to determine the percentage of time students typically spend doing (1) individual work, (2) small-group work, and (3) whole-group work. Divide and label the pie chart into appropriate portions. The second pie chart is for determining the Learning Environment. Divide it into appropriate portions of time typically spent on (1) teacher presentation; (2) class discussion; (3) group projects, labs, and explorations; and (4) individual work. To aid in making distinctions between the first two portions, teacher presentation becomes a classroom discussion when more than 50 percent of the interactions are from the students; anything less can be categorized as teacher presentation.

TIP The Learning Environment

Construct both a General Classroom Organization Chart and a Learning Environment Chart. What do these charts tell you about your teaching and learning environment? Do your charts represent your ideal environment, or do they accurately represent your instruction?

These two charts provide an overview of your classroom learning environment. Specifically, are students typically *hearing* and *seeing* content and skills, are students actively *interacting* with both the teacher and other students, are students involved in *doing* the science or mathematics, and are they individually *making sense* out of concepts? Most classes involve all these components to some degree, but the degree to which each is emphasized does vary by classroom. And it's this degree of emphasis that is central to the discussions in this book.

With an understanding of what you value and how your classroom environment is configured, let's turn to the strategies (actions) that influence learning. What instructional strategies do you typically use to teach your major concepts?

TIP Teaching Approaches

Since major concepts are not addressed on every day of instruction, think back to the last major concept or core idea that was studied as you respond to the following statements. Rate each statement based on how frequently something occurs when teaching a major concept in your classroom, using the following scale: 1, never; 2, rarely; 3, often; 4, most of the time; 5, always.

1. I teach using lecture. _____

2. My students solve open-ended problems that may have multiple correct solutions. _____

3. I teach using direct instruction. _____

4. I teach using inquiry or problem-solving strategies. _____

5. I teach concepts/skills using demonstrations or modeling. _____

6. I teach using guided practice. _____

7. My students must attempt (individually or in groups) to solve mathematical problems/scientific questions before I provide possible solution(s). _____

8. I give students the notes and information before they explore the concept. _____

9. When I teach, students are often placed in situations that require them to think critically or solve problems before the central concept is explicitly taught. _____

The statements in the TIP (above) provide a vast spectrum of teaching approaches. Some statements lean toward the teacher telling or showing information, with students memorizing or confirming information through exercises and activities (1, 3, 8). Other statements lean toward an active student role where the teacher's role becomes more of a facilitator (2, 4, 9). The remaining statements (5, 6, 7) can fall to either end of the spectrum depending on where in the lesson they occur and what precedes the activity. We may jump to conclusions or quickly try to defend one approach over the other, but the "right" answer depends on the purpose, goals, and standards that you are targeting.

For most of us, our primary experience as a K–16 student involved the teacher giving us information (often delivered by lecture and/or notes) followed by us confirming what was modeled. In mathematics, a problem set of like problems typically followed what the teacher had demonstrated on the board; and in science, an activity or confirmatory lab was provided where all the questions were asked for the student, thus minimizing critical or creative thought.

How Do You Start to Maximize Learning?

At ground level, you need to know your learners well. The degree to which you know and understand each of your students directly affects the quality of learning that will transpire in your classroom. Sure, we all want to know our learners, but how well do you really get to know each one? The interactions and relationships that you have with your students can be on many different levels. Do you know them as individuals (e.g., hobbies, interests, extracurricular involvement)? Do you know their strengths and weaknesses as a student (e.g., strong conceptually but weak in computation; strong visual learners)? Every interaction is important, but for different reasons. Knowing the student as an individual is vital for getting the student engaged in the classroom. Your interest in and knowledge of each student lets each student know you care about him or her as a person. Knowing each student's strengths and weaknesses is vital for maximizing that student's academic progress. Once you know your students' skills and aptitudes, you can better target the instruction and learning that follows.

Now that you have reflected on your teaching practice—from what you value, to what you view as critical knowledge and understandings, to the relationships that you build in your classroom—it is time to explore how your teaching aligns with inquiry-based instructional practice. You may need to make only subtle improvements to an already largely successful teaching practice, or perhaps you need to question what is truly important and then learn how to transition to a more effective inquiry-based teaching and learning environment. Regardless of your starting point, it is important to understand what inquiry is (and is not), and why it is such a critical component of effective instruction.

2

Why Inquiry,
and Why in Your Classroom?

What constitutes good teaching has been an ongoing discussion for decades. The conversation, however, has shifted from making theoretical conjectures of what *should* work in the early 1900s (Dewey, 1910, 1938), to beginning to test some of the conjectures in the 1950s and 1960s (Atkin & Karplus, 1962), to deeply analyzing the union of theory and practice to determine what *does* work (Bybee et al., 2006; Marshall, 2010). Understanding the reality of what works in various educational settings allows professional development facilitators to better target the needs of teachers and students. Additionally, cognitive science and educational psychology have been instrumental in moving the field of teacher effectiveness forward. Students need to be active participants in their learning and sense making if learning is to be optimized.

What Do We Mean by "Inquiry"?

I use the following definition of *inquiry-based instruction* in science:

> Inquiry-based instruction is the development of understanding through investigation—that is, asking questions, determining appropriate methods, gathering data, thinking critically about relationships between evidence and explanations, and formulating and communicating logical arguments. (adapted from the *National Science Education Standards*, National Research Council [NRC], 1996, p. 105)

For math teachers, *inquiry* is a less familiar term. In mathematics, you may want to think about inquiry-based instruction as the strategies that unite the process standards (e.g., problem solving, representation) with the core content (e.g., proportional reasoning, graphing).

Instruction rarely falls into absolute categories and instead typically resides along a continuum where both the teacher's and students' roles vary. The following chapters will clarify in great detail the continuum of inquiry-based instruction, but for now imagine on one end the teacher as the teller of information and the student as the recipient of information, and on the opposite end, open inquiry.

Teachers as teller → Prescriptive inquiry → Guided inquiry → Open inquiry

Extreme positions rarely provide the best approach and tend to be exclusive rather than inclusive of everyone involved. The more moderate options include prescriptive and guided forms of inquiry. Although prescriptive inquiry (also known as confirmatory or cookbook inquiry) is the most prevalent form of inquiry-based practice, students engaged in prescriptive inquiry are doing little to no critical thinking. As we will see, sometimes prescriptive inquiry is necessary, even desired, but it should be the exception and not the general procedure used. Guided inquiry is the focus of this book. When instruction includes effective guided inquiry, learning is rich, thoughtful, and challenging to students of all ability levels.

Why Inquiry Now?

Several things have been responsible for shifting the focus of instruction away from telling and more toward having students do and experience the world around them as an integral part of learning. Our societal needs have vastly changed during the last 50 years. At one time, a learned person was considered to be someone who memorized a collection of discrete facts and could perform a list of basic skills. Though much of this basic knowledge and these fundamental skills may still be important and necessary, they no longer provide the benchmark of what it means to be a learned person. A successful 21st century learner must be able to think critically, communicate ideas effectively, and collaborate with others (Partnership for 21st Century Skills, 2013). Critical thinking goes beyond a buzzword thrown around in faculty lounges or to impress parents during open house; rather, it is now imperative that students learn how to work with large data sets, design experiments, and work collaboratively to seek solutions to real-world problems that rarely have a single correct answer. The once highly esteemed fact-based knowledge that is now instantaneously available through digital media has become more of a support mechanism in the learning process instead of the final goal.

Several fundamental changes in education may help teachers move toward a greater use of inquiry-based instruction: standardized tests, standards, college-level courses, and business and industry. Currently, standardized tests and other major classroom assessments are the tail that is wagging the dog in the United States. Whether we agree with the emphasis on testing, standardized tests are changing to emphasize inquiry learning. The integrated national standards in science and mathematics (Achieve, 2013; National Governors Association Center for Best Practices & Council of Chief State School Officers, 2010) require inquiry-based instruction to be woven into the learning of core ideas; no longer can inquiry, process skills, or practices be taught as brief, isolated, irrelevant lessons. Furthermore, the newly revised goals and objectives for advanced placement (AP) college-level courses have changed the way that teachers and professors view rigorous learning. Finally, the demands and expectations of business and industry may have the greatest influence of all—even if the effect is the slowest to take place. Let's look more closely at each of these four changes.

Standardized Tests

Before you think that I have lost touch with reality, I admit that the highly fact-based standardized testing drives much of the curriculum and instruction in today's classrooms. However, I feel compelled to emphasize two things about these tests. First, many standardized tests have critical thinking or higher-order thinking embedded in their questions, so though some questions are asking for basic knowledge, many questions test students' ability to apply, analyze, and interpret.

In mathematics, the new focus on deeper, integrated learning means placing less emphasis on the actual calculation (though this is still important) and more emphasis on the application of ideas. In science, this means that defining terms and recalling facts are secondary to making observations, collecting and analyzing data, and communicating results that are supported by evidence. Major national tests such as National Assessment of Educational Progress (NAEP) and international tests like Programme for International Student Assessment (PISA) and Trends in International Mathematics and Science Study (TIMSS) have already been testing these advanced skills and modes of thinking. Many states will soon follow this trend to test higher-order, analytical thinking as national standards in math and science become fully implemented.

Standards

With the Next Generation Science Standards (2013) and the Common Core State Standards in Mathematics (2010), tests and performance assessments will continue to evaluate higher levels of thinking in the years ahead. Sure, not all states will likely embrace these national standards as they are written. Some will put their own spin on them. Regardless of whether states are working from the national standards or their own standards, each state invariably uses the national standards as a benchmark.

For the Next Generation Science Standards, each standard has a series of performance expectations that include Science and Engineering Practices, Disciplinary Core Ideas, and Crosscutting Concepts (Achieve, 2013, NRC, 2012). For instance, under the middle grade physical science standard (MS-PS1: Matter and Its Interactions), one of the six performance expectations reads, "Develop models to describe the atomic composition of simple molecules and extended structures." This performance expectation is central to the study of two core ideas from the framework (NRC, 2012): the structure and properties of matter, and chemical reactions. Under the former National Science Education Standards (NRC, 1996), learning about the structure of matter was a lower-level pursuit. Now, the NGSS example shows that for students to achieve mastery, it becomes essential, not just recommended, that inquiry forms of learning become seamlessly joined with learning the content surrounding the atomic composition of molecules.

The Common Core State Standards for Mathematics describe the standards for mathematical practice or the processes and proficiencies that students must master (National Governors Association Center for Best Practices & Council of Chief State School Officers, 2010). The processes and proficiencies are based on work from the National Council of Teachers of Mathematics (NCTM, 2000) process standards that include *problem solving, reasoning and proof, communication, representation,* and *connections.* In addition, the proficiencies are based on the work of an NRC (2001) report that includes *adaptive reasoning, strategic competence, conceptual understanding, procedural fluency,* and *productive disposition.* Although the term *inquiry-based instruction* is not prevalent in mathematics conversations, the descriptors in italics here used for processes and proficiencies provide a rich account of what occurs in classrooms that are rich in inquiry-based instruction and learning.

Taken together, the elements that compose the processes and proficiencies support a student's ability to learn and apply more demanding math concepts and procedures. The middle school and high school standards call on students to practice applying mathematical ways of thinking to real-world issues and challenges; to achieve mastery for a given standard requires students to think and reason mathematically. The Common Core State Standards set a rigorous definition of college and career readiness, not by piling topic upon topic, but by demanding that students develop a depth of understanding and ability to apply mathematics to novel situations, as college students and employees in a highly skilled workforce regularly do.

College-Level Courses

The College Board, which organizes the AP course structure through which students can earn college credit for taking advanced classes, has overhauled what rigorous learning looks like. The old approach was predicated on covering massive amounts of material through lecture and directed or confirmatory laboratory investigations—the "drinking out of a fire hose" approach to learning where students are exposed to tremendous amounts of material typically at the expense of deep conceptual understanding. The new course objectives in AP Biology and AP Chemistry (among others) explicitly state that teachers should reduce the breadth of content in an effort to promote conceptual understanding. In addition, teachers are to emphasize scientific inquiry and student-directed labs, which is a move away from the previous lecture-and-demonstration model of learning to a more collaborative, inquiry-focused, explorative environment. Although not all schools and students are directly involved in AP courses, this shift from simple coverage to deeper understanding as an instructional emphasis is important for everyone because these courses have long stood as benchmarks for what rigorous learning entails. So, instructional leaders should begin to see that rigor is about depth of understanding and the ability to apply core ideas to other learning situations. For decades, honors and advanced classes in elementary schools through college have been based on covering material faster. Now deep, thoughtful learning trumps shallow, high-speed coverage.

Business and Industry

Approximately 100 years ago, John Dewey stated that school often gets in the way of learning (Dewey, 1910, 1938). His views on education have continued to guide effective teaching and learning to this day. Part of this vision included espousing that schools need to better represent the real world. Contemporary business and industry leaders agree. In presentation after presentation, they make it clear that students need much more than just content to excel.

Great jobs continue to go unfilled around the United States because students are lacking collaborative skills and problem-solving aptitude. As our country continues to struggle through a recession, I hear that employers are looking to hire but find that applicants do not possess the required skill set. BMW, for instance, has more than a dozen high-paying engineering positions that are currently unfilled at its South Carolina plant. According to a 2012 reporting from the area chamber of commerce leader, upstate South Carolina has scores of unfilled high-skilled positions.

If we have marginally qualified teachers in science and mathematics classrooms, teaching will be solely about coverage, learning in these disciplines will be about difficult-to-understand material far removed from students' real-world experience, and students will be unengaged. Helping students envision a future in great careers requires the guidance of engaging teachers who can begin to reverse the trend. This requires having students *do* science and mathematics—not just read about these subjects or be told about them.

Why Inquiry in Your Classroom?

So why should you move toward an inquiry-based, intentional vision that incorporates research and practice? To answer that question, ask yourself another one: regardless of whether you feel equipped to facilitate a particular strategy, how do your students learn best—and why?

I tend to shy away from blanket answers, but I confidently say that you should include inquiry-based instruction when teaching major concepts or core ideas in science or mathematics. Numerous studies have continued to confirm that both short- and long-term learning of major ideas is better achieved through guided inquiry learning than more traditional didactic or direct instruction approaches (Blanchard et al., 2010; Wilson, Taylor, Kowalski, & Carlson, 2009). Furthermore, research has shown that students of science teachers leading inquiry-based instruction perform better than a virtual comparison group of like students who received more traditional instruction (Marshall, 2012). These results are true for both content and process knowledge. Advocates for direct instruction over inquiry often are comparing direct instruction to open inquiry or discovery learning approaches. Open inquiry and discovery learning suffer in comparison because they lack needed focus. Chapter 6 will clearly define and clarify the target of guided inquiry-based instruction.

Why do students often learn better in successful guided inquiry environments?

First, to truly learn a major concept, the information needs to be moved beyond short-term memory into long-term memory, and inquiry is effective in providing the repeated exposure and scaffolding necessary to support long-term memory development. Major concepts or core ideas should be revisited in many ways during the year and should be tied to other major ideas. These core ideas and concepts must be integral to many class discussions, activities, and learning objectives. As you help develop conceptual understanding that becomes part of a student's long-term memory, you are also reducing the cognitive load on the learner, which frees up short-term memory to process and assimilate new ideas and information without being overwhelming. Plus, the deeper tie to memory will allow the learner, in the future, to build multiple permanent connections to these foundational understandings.

Other research on the brain underscores the role of rigorous, meaningful learning in the development of the brain's neural connections. Children's brains have immense plasticity, and our efforts as teachers are either developing (strengthening) or breaking (pruning) our students' neural connections (Willis, 2006). When students passively take notes, complete low-level tasks and activities, spout back rote facts with no connections to their real life or prior knowledge, or simply confirm what they have been told, their brains are actively trimming (pruning) unnecessary neural connections—an anti-learning of sorts.

Another way inquiry-focused instruction benefits students is through its dynamic makeup of brief, engaging chunks of material. Learners in middle grades have a typical attention span for listening of about 15 minutes (a bit less for elementary students and a bit more for high school students). Thus, listening, taking notes, or copying teacher solutions for long periods of time is not particularly beneficial to the learner (though it is easiest on the teacher). I'm betting this point comes as no surprise, but it still is a common occurrence in classrooms. Perhaps the best balance results from being intentional about the instructional decision and basing the decisions on your goals. Do you want students to work with the content, thinking and questioning (analyzing a data set), or do you just need them to remember facts?

The teacher who uses only lecture and demonstration cannot hope to elicit much beyond a recall of facts from her students, and thus learning is not maximized when studying core ideas. Since long-term academic success is largely dependent on students' engagement, it makes sense that we build our learning environments so that students are thinking, analyzing, creating, and exploring—to name a few of the higher-order skills that guided inquiry-based learning encourages.

2

Details of
INQUIRY
Instruction

3

What Framework Supports Effective Inquiry-Based Practice?

Imagine you decide to take a trip with your family to enjoy the beauty of fall in New England. Such a trip requires a significant amount of planning—for example, which highways to take, where to stay, what sites to visit along the way, and how to beat the crowds during peak tourist season.

Effective teaching requires a similar need for planning. Although your teaching goals or objectives may be unique, you still need to consider what you expect from all students (objectives), how you will achieve success with all students (the lesson), and to what degree you were successful (formative and summative assessments). This chapter gives you a map for arriving at high-quality inquiry-based instruction.

If your class is studying energy, for example, you can scour the Internet for activities and lessons on energy (29 million possibilities, the last time I checked), implement the lesson, and then create a grade for each student to put into your grade book. Or you could use some of those activities to systematically devise a plan that ties today's lesson with students' prior experiences and progress in a manner that challenges student thinking while building conceptual understanding. This second option—the focus of this chapter—has the greater chance of improving student achievement among all learners.

The Need for an Instructional Framework

Most teachers realize that they must incorporate a myriad of instructional approaches into their classes to effectively reach all students. However, most teachers also get little guidance on how to successfully assimilate the best practices in the classroom. In addition, a teacher's beliefs plus mandates dictated by the department, school, and district also frame the specific instructional approach for a lesson or unit. Attending to these various and typically competing demands often results in a piecemeal approach to adopting and implementing various instructional initiatives.

If teachers are to adopt inquiry-based instruction as a significant instructional approach, they need a framework to support their efforts. Such a framework must be coherent enough to combine the many things that we know about good instruction and also dynamic enough to adapt to the various instructional settings found in classrooms around the nation. The 4E × 2 (read "4E by 2") Instructional Model, shown in Figure 3.1, unites three major components of learning that have each separately been shown to improve student learning:

- Inquiry-based instruction, with four phases (Engage, Explore, Explain, and Extend)
- Formative assessment
- Teacher reflective practice

Repeatedly shown to be critical aspects of instruction, formative assessment and reflective practice are explicitly incorporated into each stage of inquiry in the 4E × 2 model (Atkin & Karplus, 1962; Bybee et al., 2006; Marshall, Horton, & Smart, 2009). The resulting synergy of best practices improves teacher effectiveness as well as teacher efficiency. Let's explore the importance of formative assessment and teacher reflective practice in more depth.

Formative Assessment: Continually Checking In with Students

Formative assessment encompasses both the data that you collect from students during instruction and your actions based on your interpretation of these data. Why is formative assessment so critical? Because rather than waiting to help struggling students until it is too late (e.g., at the end of a chapter, the unit, or a long lesson), you can use formative assessment to make informed decisions at each step in the instructional process. In other words, you determine whether students have grasped the material and are ready to move on, or whether they need some type of review or remediation. An important reminder: formative assessment is only effective when teachers intentionally *act* on the data that they gather from students in order to improve instruction. When formative assessments become an integral component of instruction, student achievement increases (Black & Wiliam, 1998; Marzano, 2006).

TIP Formative Assessment

Think about the degree to which your instructional practice is guided by formative assessments. Is it occasional, almost by accident when it happens? Or is it central to your daily interactions with students? How do you use the *student* data from formative assessments in your instruction? One idea that will be revisited later is to check in with all students at least two to three times each class period using high-value formative assessments.

Chapters 4 and 5 present lessons with descriptions of high-value formative assessments, but here I will quickly distinguish between high-value and low-value formative assessments. Low-value formative assessments (e.g., "Please raise your hand if you got 3.25 for exercise 3") do not offer meaningful information about student success or learning. They only measure the surface understanding—was the answer correct? A high-value formative assessment might include students discussing in small groups their specific approaches to solving the most challenging homework exercise. If they didn't come to a solution, then what questions do they still have that need to be addressed? The teacher would chat with the small groups to see where confusion, understanding, and misconceptions arose. These interactions and the class discussion that follows would provide excellent data for the teacher to know where he needs to tweak or even completely restructure instruction to maximize conceptual understanding. Granted, more low-value formative assessments can be asked in a class period, but to what end? They rarely, if ever, improve instruction or learning.

Figure 3.1
4E × 2 Instructional Model

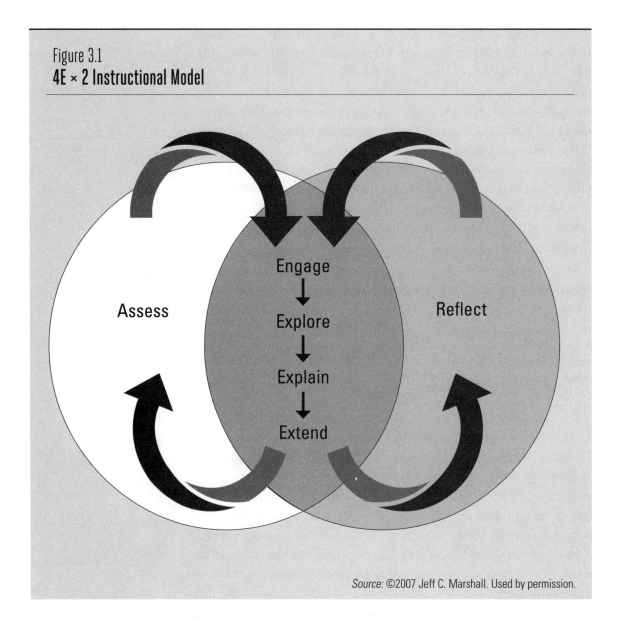

Source: ©2007 Jeff C. Marshall. Used by permission.

Teacher Reflective Practice—Now Where?

You have facilitated lessons that have succeeded as well as some that have flopped. Are your successful days due to chance or intentionality? Could you recreate that success (or avoid the flop) on an upcoming lesson?

Teachers must reflect often and deeply on their practice if they are to improve instruction; without such reflective practice, teachers will not grow. Reflective practice involves looking back and evaluating the degree of success of the instruction, classroom interactions, and learning that occurred (Shepardson & Britsch, 2001; Wilson & Clarke, 2004). The National Board for Professional Teaching Standards (NBPTS) bases certification largely on the demonstrated abilities of teachers to reflect deeply and critically over their own practice (NBPTS, 1994, 2000, 2006).

A teacher's reflective practice couples nicely with the formative assessments she conducts in the classroom. Furthermore, formative assessment and reflective practice provide a guide for improved teacher intentionality and deeper student self-awareness. When students become more self-aware of their learning (often referred to as *metacognition*), they are better able to ask questions and seek solutions for points that are unclear or confusing—which in turn results in fewer blank stares or "I don't know" statements from students. Instead, students become better able to articulate their strengths and weaknesses as a learner (e.g., "I understand what the problem is asking, but I'm confused about the steps involved in the calculation").

The 4E × 2 Instructional Model

Figure 3.1 (p. 30) shows how the three major learning components entailed in the model interrelate. Although all four components of inquiry—Engage, Explore, Explain, and Extend—may not necessarily be present in a given lesson, students must have an opportunity to explore the major concepts and then engage in the Explain phase for high-quality inquiry to occur.

Teachers often ask me, "How and when do I provide my notes, lecture, and practice materials for students?" After students have had an opportunity to explore an idea—say, motion or force in a science class—it is appropriate to provide notes or a lecture. In switching the order from Explain-Explore to Explore-Explain, you and the students will quickly realize a difference: notes or a lecture becomes a summary of what has been learned rather than the central aspect to learning. Furthermore, after students have had the Explore-Explain experience, they can practice problems related to the concept. Textbook or worksheet problem sets now have meaning and value related to the explored concepts.

TIP 4E × 2 Overview

It is easy to just read through each of the 4E components without taking time to process what it means for your classroom, so after reading each "E" discussion, pause and answer the following questions (just replace the word *Engage* with the proper E component for each stage—Explore, Explain, Extend):

1. What are the major components of Engage?

2. What are examples of specific questions that you would ask during the Engage portion of learning?

3. Describe assessments that you can use or have used to assess student formative understanding during the Engage phase.

4. How could you tweak a past or future lesson to include an Engage component?

Here is a closer look at the sequence of phases that provides an opportunity for students to explore a concept before we explain it.

Engage

Most of the teachers I work with at first equate Engage strictly with motivation. Engaging the learner through a hook, mind capture, or perturbation does effectively initiate the learning process, but engaging students in inquiry-based learning is more involved than just considering student motivation. In the model, the Engage phase of inquiry includes all of the following aspects:

- Probing prior knowledge,
- Identifying alternatives or misconceptions,
- Providing motivation and interest-inducing stimuli, and
- Developing scientific questioning (fundamental to both science and math classes).

Teacher intentionality is critical for determining the degree that each aspect is emphasized in a given lesson. For instance, if the lesson or unit is inherently highly motivating, then you might best spend your time focusing on revealing students' prior knowledge or misconceptions.

Effective questioning is critical during all phases of inquiry-based learning. Effective questions to guide teacher facilitation during the four aspects of the Engage phase include the following questions.

- What do you know about ___?
- What have you seen like this?
- What have you heard about ___ that you aren't sure is true?
- What would you like to investigate regarding ___?

TIP Engage and Your Teaching

In an effort to link Engage to your teaching, write two or more questions that represent aspects associated with the Engage phase of instruction (e.g., your student's prior knowledge, motivation, and misconceptions).

Intentional, effective questioning is necessary, but not sufficient on its own, to determine if students are ready to proceed to the Explore phase, need a quick review, or need remediation before they can investigate the topic further. Formative assessments can provide content-rich scenarios to check your students' understanding and help to decide when to move on in the unit. Formative assessments for the Engage phase might include a discrepant event (i.e., a surprising or startling science demonstration that powerfully piques students' curiosity), a pre-test to gauge misconceptions, formative probes (Keeley, Eberle, & Farrin, 2005), or KWHL charts (van Zee, Iwasyk, Kurose, Simpson, & Wild, 2001). A KWHL chart is a graphic organizer that facilitates learning by having students answer the following questions:

1. What do I *know*?
2. What do I *want* to know?
3. *How* do I find out?
4. What have I *learned*?

The more commonly known KWL chart leaves out a fundamental step for science and mathematics education that asks students to articulate *how* the investigation and learning will take place—for example, designing a procedure in science or a solution path in mathematics.

Integrating formative assessments into the Engage phase of the inquiry framework gives you a robust model for involving students in the three primary learning outcomes for inquiry-based teaching: conceptual understanding, the ability to perform scientific inquiry or mathematical reasoning, and an understanding about inquiry (NRC, 2000). Such assessments also require students to think metacognitively—thus making them aware of their own thinking. This way of thinking helps you become more intentional about your practice and encourage students to become invested in their own learning. In time, this process will help raise the achievement of all students—especially those who are low performing (Black & Wiliam, 1998; NRC, 2000).

When teachers reflect on what has occurred during the Engage stage, they gain valuable information that informs their decisions for the next steps of instructional practice. For instance, by asking yourself, "What did my students' prior knowledge tell me about their readiness to learn?" you are challenged to address specific student needs before plowing through more material. It may become evident that a group of students or even the whole class needs some remediation before proceeding. Another option is for you to address a deficit area (e.g., interpreting a graph, understanding energy conversions) as the lesson proceeds but before it is completed. Regardless of which path you choose, you now are making decisions based on data, with the intention of doing whatever is best to improve your students' learning. This approach is in sharp contrast to simply covering material and then finding out at the end of the unit that 60 percent or more of the class failed to understand the fundamental concept being studied—a frustrating outcome for the teacher and students alike. Instead, reflective practice allows teaching to be specific and targeted to students' needs.

Explore

Once you and your class have successfully navigated the Engage stage, you can lead students into the Explore phase. Note, however, that sometimes you might omit the Engage stage. For instance, if a previous lesson in the unit uncovered the students' prior knowledge, or if the goals of the Engage and Explore phases can be collapsed into one instructional activity, then you may begin a lesson with Explore. Regardless of whether it is the first or second component of the lesson, Explore is a necessary and vital component of all successful inquiry learning experiences. The key aspects that define Explore include actively involving students in one or more of the following activities: predicting, designing, testing, collecting, and reasoning (Achieve, 2013; NGA Center & CCSSO, 2010; National Research Council, 2012).

TIP Explore

Effective questions that help guide students through the Explore phase include the following:

- What if…?
- How can you best study this question or problem?
- What happens when…?
- What information do you need to collect?
- Why did you choose your method to study the question or problem?
- Pause now to write at least two more questions that you might ask during this phase of instruction.

Like their roles in the Engage phase, formative assessment and reflective practice are essential for keeping students directed along a meaningful learning path. The assessments can be contextualized into knowledge- or process-centered domains that focus on the individual, small groups, or whole class. Furthermore, formative assessment and reflective practice become meaningfully intertwined when individual responses are united with small- and large-group discussions. A common example is the think-pair-share learning strategy (Lyman, 1981).

Often teachers limit themselves to a fairly passive observational role when assessing student progress during Explore. Although it may be beneficial to let students wade in the muck at times, you may want to assume a more active role by providing guided prompts to encourage individuals or groups to think more deeply about the investigation at hand. For instance, you could ask groups of students to describe the procedure that they intend to follow, and then have them tell you how this approach will help answer the study question. Doing so encourages students to slow down and think about how they interact with the content and what their thought processes are. In addition, having students assess their own progress in real time gives you critical information to guide intentional instruction (Tobias & Everson, 2000) and excellent opportunities to deliver differentiated instruction (Tomlinson, 2003).

TIP Rethinking Your Lessons

Think of two investigations for which your students could devise their own procedure or approach, even if they need a scaffold. With what concepts would this approach be advantageous, and what concepts would require a different strategy?

Reflective practice during the Explore phase may begin by reviewing individual student entries in science or math journals or by considering students' proficiency in responding to their completion of the H portion of the KWHL chart ("How do I effectively study this question or problem?"). For example, if you learn that data collection seems problematic for your science class, then you might initiate a brief discussion with small groups that focuses on how to gather data in meaningful ways. Such interactions with students emphasize assessment *for* learning instead of assessment *of* learning. Note that students play a pivotal role in teacher reflection. In the Explore phase, for example, the teacher should reflect on questions such as "How successful were students in setting up a scientific study? How meaningful were the data that they collected? How well are students able to justify and defend their approach?"

At this point, I hope you see that formative assessment and reflective practice have considerable overlap. In fact, when formative assessment and reflective practice merge, instruction is intentional and purposeful. More important, students are continually updated on their progress in relation to their goals (Marzano, 2006; Stiggins, 2005; Tobias & Everson, 2000).

Uniting inquiry-based instruction, formative assessment, and reflective practice during the Explore phase intentionally encourages deeper understanding. All three components are central throughout the instructional process, and the students and teacher no longer have to wait until the end of the investigation before knowing whether students truly "get it" (Black & Wiliam, 1998; Wiggins & McTighe, 2005).

Explain

As dynamic as the 4E × 2 model is, its framework is predicated on the Explore phase preceding the Explain phase. This order minimizes teacher-centered, confirmatory learning, which is often superficial.

Instead, an Explore-before-Explain approach demands a student-centered learning environment. During the Explain phase, students begin to make sense of how their prior knowledge and alternative conceptions from the Engage phase align with findings from the Explore phase. This sense making occurs when students begin to communicate results and evidence (NRC, 2012). However, if explanation precedes exploration—which is typical in instruction that is not inquiry-based—students are thrust into passive learning situations that rarely challenge them to confront misconceptions or gaps in prior knowledge. So, when Explore precedes Explain, inquiry and content can be combined in highly engaging ways that help students reshape their previous conceptions to align with their new learning (Carin, Bass, & Contant, 2005).

During Explore, process skills are emphasized as students grapple with ideas. Then content becomes central during the Explain phase as the process skills are used to support higher-order thinking such as interpreting, justifying, and analyzing. In this Explore-before-Explain model, students from diverse backgrounds and with diverse abilities now have shared experiences as a basis for their claims and ideas. Other prior experiences that students bring to class enrich the learning, too, but learning is accessible to all students because the data collected and observations made were experienced by everyone in class. At the core of the Explain phase— and inquiry learning in general—students are involved in a recursive cycle between evidence and explanations. Ideally, the practices (or process skills) and content become embedded in the investigation.

TIP Explain

Central aspects of the Explain phase include (1) interpreting data and findings; (2) providing evidence for claims; (3) communicating findings (written, oral, using technology); and (4) providing alternative explanations for findings. Effective questions you can pose during this phase include the following:

- What pattern(s) did you notice?

- What evidence do you have for your claims?

- How can you best explain or show your findings?

- What are some other explanations for your findings?

What additional questions could you use during the Explain phase?

Assessments for the Explain phase include lab reports, presentations, and discussions. These assessments can be formative or summative depending on the implementation. If you allow students to resubmit work or ask them to revise their work based on peer editing, then assessment becomes formative, emphasizing the learning process over the learning product. Rubrics should be clear in their requirements but also flexible to allow for the unique expression of ideas. The goal is for students to understand concepts that are embedded within scientific or mathematical inquiries, not for them to fill out a worksheet properly. If interpreting data and providing evidence are central to a particular investigation, then students need to justify their claims using the documented data and results.

Improved learning has been noted when both formative assessment and metacognition are used to guide students (Bransford, Brown, & Cocking, 2000; Costa & Kallick, 2000). Metacognitive strategies create time for sense making, when students can reconcile their new knowledge with their prior knowledge. At the same time, the teacher is gathering valuable information to improve instruction. Furthermore, as students become mindful of their own learning, they start to use those strategies that assist their own progress. Graphic organizers such as KWHL charts and POE (predict, observe, explain) cycles (White & Gunstone, 1992) that may have been started during earlier phases can now be completed (e.g., "What have you learned? Explain your results."). Concept maps can be used in a new way during the Explain phase: during Engage, they highlight knowledge gaps whereas during Explain, they illustrate links among new concepts, prior knowledge, and learned skills.

Reflective practice during the Explain phase entails the teacher considering points such as "How strong are the claims being made by the student? How well are students able to convey knowledge of key concepts? How accurate are their claims?" During the Explain phase, students begin to unite their prior knowledge with their investigation. Although teachers should have a basic expectation for minimum performance for all students, they also should challenge students to exceed this expectation according to their interests and backgrounds—a point in the lesson that offers an excellent opportunity for differentiated instruction.

Teachers often are confused regarding how and where student practice and teacher explanation should occur in inquiry lessons. First, both of these elements are critical to complete sense making and automation of skills, so it is a matter of when, not if. In inquiry where Explore precedes Explain, teachers still will find the need to clarify, explain, and draw the pieces together. Such a discussion fits nicely toward the end of Explain, after students have grappled with ideas. In addition, teachers find that what previously may have been a 40-minute lecture now becomes a 10- to 15-minute review, and students often need more practice with the concept, algorithm, or idea—or what mathematics teachers often refer to as skill automation or computational fluency. Now is the time for this critical practice to occur—after students have explored the idea and have an understanding of the concept or equation.

Extend

The Extend phase plays a critical role in effective inquiry instruction. If learning is not reinforced and then internalized after Explain, when conceptual understanding begins to take hold, then students may quickly revert back to prior knowledge and the understandings (and possibly misconceptions) they had before the investigation. Providing one or more opportunities for students to apply their knowledge in meaningful, authentic contexts during the Extend phase helps students solidify their conceptual understanding and develop a more permanent mental representation.

Misconceptions are hard to revise and must be repeatedly addressed before lasting change occurs (Hestenes, Wells, & Swackhamer, 1992). Now, in the Extend phase, the mental disequilibrium students experienced during Engage and Explore begins to shift as the understanding and knowledge expressed during Explain are applied to both new situations and prior concepts. You can determine the number of Extend activities or the amount of time for this phase by considering the difficulty of the concept(s) being studied, the concept's importance in the curriculum, and the degree of understanding shown by all students.

TIP Extend

During Extend, students are asked to apply, elaborate, transfer, and generalize knowledge to novel situations. Appropriate questions for the Extend phase include the following:

- How do you think _____ applies to _____?

- What would happen if…?

- Where can we use this concept in the real world?

- What consequences, benefits, and risks will come with certain decisions?

What other questions can you use with your students in an upcoming lesson?

At this point in the inquiry process, assessments typically are seen only as summative. However, by providing formative assessment during Extend, you can encourage students to think more deeply about their work. For example, you might split students into small teams to perform a new investigation or to solve a new problem that remains focused on the main concepts being studied. Or ask students to reflect in their journals on an area of weakness that you observed during a presentation.

Reflective practice is designed to address explicitly whether the content has been mastered or still needs work. This strategy, of course, can give you valuable information as you decide what to do next and how to improve future instruction. During the Extend phase, students should have an opportunity to deepen their cognition and solidify their knowledge on a given concept. In this stage of inquiry, you want to understand to what degree students are successful in transferring knowledge to new ideas and the quality of understanding that students can demonstrate. Reflective practice in this stage of instruction really is focusing on the degree of conceptual understanding. The importance of the concept to the subject will help you determine the level of proficiency and the depth of understanding to expect from all students.

Dynamic Variations of the Model

On first glance of the 4E × 2 model, you may find it logical to proceed sequentially through the phases, having students demonstrate their knowledge and understanding and moving along to the next concept. Conceptual understanding, however, does not always follow such a linear, straightforward path. Just as there is not one scientific method (Windschitl, 2003), the 4E × 2 model's dynamic structure supports more than one approach. You may opt to vary from the model's progression through Engage, Explore, Explain, and Extend, but your decision should be guided by following whatever path best supports your students' strong conceptual development.

As I stated earlier, the one consistent tip is that Explore should always precede Explain. That said, several variations of the model are possible, each with a clear rationale.

Variation 1: Multiple Extensions

Engage-Explore-Explain-n (Extend) is the default or typical path expressed by the 4E × 2 Instructional Model. The n denotes that multiple Extend opportunities should be encouraged. The decision for how many, exactly, is based on (1) the depth of student knowledge conveyed thus far; (2) where in the unit or theme the Extend investigation occurs; (3) the relative importance of concepts, standards, and skills to the overall goals for the course; and (4) whether prior content, skills, and ideas that have been studied can be embedded into the essential focus of the investigation. So, if students understand at a significant level and can apply the knowledge to several different situations, then you can confidently move forward to a new concept or idea. If you have introduced a new concept that will be reinforced later by another, related activity, then you may want to opt to minimize the number of Extend opportunities. However, if your students are not likely to see this information again, then employing several Extend opportunities makes sense. Likewise, if several concepts throughout the course overlap with the current concept being studied, then multiple Extend opportunities are useful.

Variation 2: Multiple Explore-Explain Cycles

Another variation, in a science or a math class, is to begin with Engage and then lead three consecutive cycles of Explore-Explain before implementing a final Extend. This approach is useful when your class is studying three closely related ideas. For instance, displacement, velocity, and acceleration could be studied in three different investigations before students transfer their prior and current learning (Extend) to motion in general.

Variation 3: Multiple Explores

A third variation entails Engage-Explore1-Explore2-Explore3-Explain-Extend. This approach is applicable when students are exploring one scientific question or mathematical idea several ways before they explain their findings. For instance, students could investigate three different plant types before seeking to apply what they studied to a larger ecosystem application. In a math class, students might study the patterns they find by exploring three different linear contexts before they try to explain their findings. Note that in these examples, Engage was used only during the initial iteration because alternative conceptions should be clearly known and continually addressed during subsequent investigations.

Concluding Thoughts

The three learning constructs—inquiry-based instruction, formative assessment, and reflective practice—included in the 4E × 2 Instructional Model all have a positive impact on teaching and learning (Black & Wiliam, 1998; Bybee et al., 2006; Tobias & Everson, 2000). Unifying the constructs into one coherent model lets teachers focus their instructional practice on these core fundamentals, improving their practice. While the 4E × 2 model is a dynamic inquiry-based instructional model, it also reminds us of the importance and interrelationship among these three essential learning constructs.

Although the model does not address everything we need to know about effective practice, it provides a meaningful, coherent structure to help teachers plan, implement, and assess their instruction. Teachers using this model may need to devote significant time, at least initially, to lesson planning, but I am confident that the result of deeper, more meaningful learning will pay dividends in the long run. Also, the time required for planning decreases dramatically as inquiry-based instruction becomes more familiar. A dynamic web tool (www.clemson.edu/iim/lessonplans) provides standards-based lessons and a template to help teachers create new lessons. Chapter 4 and 5 also describe several examples of lessons and units that incorporate the model in science and mathematics settings.

4

Inquiry Exemplars:
How Does a Lesson Look and Feel?

In Chapter 1, you explored your teaching values and practice. In Chapter 2, you learned why inquiry is such a vital aspect of successful teaching and learning. In Chapter 3, you were introduced to a model that unites inquiry, formative assessment, and reflective practice. Now it is time to fold these three topics together in examining specific examples of inquiry-based lessons for science and mathematics that use the 4E × 2 Instructional Model. The science lessons here are based on the Next Generation Science Standards, and the math lessons are based on the Common Core State Standards for Mathematics.

Every lesson in this chapter follows the same format: key concept, national standard, objective, essential question, and then you are given a contextual setting in the lesson overview. Following that, the 4E × 2 instructional path gives a concise overview of each component (e.g., Explore), followed by a detailed Teacher Support section to assist with actual implementation of that inquiry phase. Although the primary audience is middle and high school teachers, sections called Adaptations describe how the lesson can be altered for different audiences and age groups, as well as what nuances teachers need to keep in mind to be fully effective with the content or concept.

The eight inquiry-based lessons here are ready to be implemented, but I hope they inspire you to reflect further on your teaching for the other 175 or so days of the school year. When combined with thoughtful reflection or conversation with peers, these examples will help you tweak current instructional plans to model Explore before Explain and integrate formative assessments throughout instruction. The goal is not to scrap everything that you now do. Rather, in most cases, you will simply become more intentional and focused. This means transforming your current activities, notes, or worksheets that just cover a topic into more meaningful experiences that deeply engage your students in learning and that focus on the core ideas to promote conceptual understanding. It is not enough to say, "Here are the notes—learn them." We must challenge our students to think, set high yet manageable expectations, and offer the support and scaffolding necessary to help raise students to high levels of performance.

Explain and Confirm Paradigm

Before examining the eight example lessons, let's look at a generic Explain-before-Explore practice—the more common instructional modus operandi. Explain-before-Explore instruction typically follows the following path: *(1) Review: Teacher reviews previous problems or homework.* Students may give answers or even write work on the board, but the teacher typically focuses on correctness and then moves along. *(2) Introduce: Teacher introduces a new concept.* Often with little or no context given, the teacher shares a new concept, through lecture or demonstration. *(3) Model: Teacher models the concept or problem solution with one or more examples.* Students follow along during this typically abstract telling of information. *(4) Practice: Students practice the concept through homework or verify through a prescriptive lab.* The goal is for students to be able to replicate solution methods or to parrot what was told to them.

You may say, "I've done Explain before Explore (or even just Explain) for years, and it hasn't harmed students yet." Or has it? As I work with teachers, I hear about a lot of students who are failing. We need to look beyond just bad home lives to understand what prevents these students from progressing. In addition, for students who are doing well, how are you challenging them to think deeply every day about science or mathematics in the Explain-first approach?

Explore-First Paradigm

The Explore-before-Explain approach generally follows this pattern.

1. Engage: Teacher identifies students' prior knowledge and misconceptions (possibly through a warm-up, short quiz, or engaging question or activity). The goal is not to resolve any misconceptions but, rather, to set the stage to work content so that misconceptions are resolved or new learning occurs.

2. Explore: Students explore the content (through a guided inquiry experience that is facilitated by the teacher). Material and notes are not frontloaded. Students must work with the environment, motion, graphs, data, or problems before concepts (e.g., photosynthesis, slope) are discussed and understood. Students come into the lesson, curious to understand the world and to solve authentic problems that involve science and mathematics. The teacher provides the context to allow concepts like photosynthesis and slope to become meaningful and necessary, not just things to memorize.

3. Explain: Students and teacher explain the concept (through discussions, explanations, notes, and presentations). In this sense-making stage, misconceptions begin to be resolved, the teacher shares notes to help clarify, and students justify solutions and defend answers. Although sense making occurs, ideas are loosely held at this point.

4. Extend: Students continue to work with the concept (continuing to explore, practicing computational fluency, and applying to previous ideas and concepts). Practice and application of ideas are critical so that learning is deeply rooted and practiced.

Sample Science Lessons

The following sample science lessons are offered to show how you might teach an Explore-before-Explain lesson in your classroom. Math lessons are offered after this section.

Science Lesson 1: Bob the Drinking Bird

Key Concepts: Gas laws; conservation of energy

Next Generation Science Standard: MS-PS3/HS-PS3 Energy

Objective: Students will reason through and explain how the bird continues to bob.

Essential Question: Will Bob the Drinking Bird continue to bob forever?

Lesson Overview: This lesson uses an inexpensive toy (two for $10) that is available from scientific supply companies and toy stores. Students seek to discover what factors cause Bob to continue bobbing into the water glass. On the surface, this demonstration seems to model perpetual motion (which is not possible). Students should eventually realize through exploration that the water that Bob dips into is the energy source. Once the energy source is removed, the cycle will slow and then eventually stop.

Engage: Give a 6- to 10-question true/false pretest to reveal any misconceptions held regarding the gas laws or conservation of energy. A student explanation should accompany any false response. A quiz provides a nice diagnostic assessment to begin the lesson. Sample questions might include "If an object is stationary, then it does not have any energy" (false—it can have one or more forms of stored potential energy) and "The density of a gas increases inside a closed rigid container when the temperature increases" (false—pressure increases, but the volume and mass are left unchanged).

Teacher Support for Engage: The goal of the pretest is to identify misconceptions and areas where knowledge is weak. Don't try to have students resolve all the answers here. Instead, have students discuss where they were confused or uncertain. The Explore experience will help students address misconceptions, thus resolving content errors through experience, not memorization.

Explore: Through a series of probing questions, students work in groups of two to three to explore how Bob bobs in the water. Bob seems to defy gravity as the liquid goes up the tube. How can this be?

Teacher Support for Explore: The goal during Explore is to challenge students' thinking without allowing students to become frustrated to the point of shutting down and disengaging. Some questions that help guide the groups in their thinking might include "Does the liquid have any effect on Bob continuing to bob?"; "Describe what occurs inside the tube after Bob bobs"; "What causes the liquid to move up the tube?"; "How does getting Bob's head wet affect the bobbing cycle?" Initially, let the students use their own wording, such as "The liquid is sucked up in the tube"; later, during the Explain phase, you can help students replace misleading terms like *sucked up*.

Explain: Students create a four-block cartoon strip using no more than 30 words to explain how Bob continues to bob. Though it may be possible to explain the phenomenon accurately in other ways, terms like *gas pressure, evaporation, fulcrum,* and *lever* will likely show up in the students' cartoons, depending on conversations had during the explore phase. Groups rotate around the room to see if other students have provided an accurate, clear explanation.

Teacher Support for Explain: One possible explanation is that as Bob dips into the water, evaporation begins on the exterior of the head, causing the gas inside the head to cool. As the gas in the upper chamber cools, the pressure inside the tube decreases. The gas pressure in the bottom chamber remains the same, but its relative pressure is now greater than that in the top chamber. Thus, the liquid is forced up the tube, creating an imbalance in the tube that in turn causes Bob to bob. The cycle then begins all over again. The water is the energy source, so as long as water continues to be available, Bob will continue bobbing (unless the relative humidity surrounding the toy becomes too great).

This toy does not demonstrate perpetual motion (although it may seem so to the students) because water (the energy source) needs to continue to be supplied. Students tend to say that the liquid inside the bird is "sucked up" into its head. Begin the discussion, in Engage, with the words and phrases that the students use; but now with the Explain phase in progress, question students further and correct them as necessary so that proper vocabulary is introduced and used when students are ready. For instance, you might say, "Although the water looks like it's getting sucked up into the tube, we know that water flows from higher pressure to lower pressure."

Extend: Students create, test, and then explain what factors would change the rate of Bob's bob (e.g., higher humidity, a different liquid that Bob bobs into, or increased evaporation with a fan). Students should first make a detailed prediction. Then, when possible, they should test their prediction. Student teams will share their findings. Revisit the pretest of common misconceptions to see if students have improved their understanding.

Teacher Support for Extend: Whether gas laws or conservation of energy is the focus, the Extend phase gives students an opportunity to further apply their knowledge and deepen their understanding, which may be tentative. The movement of the liquid up the tube can be compared with drinking out of a straw. It is a puzzle for students to figure out how liquid is forced up through a straw into one's mouth instead of being "sucked" in. (As the diaphragm pulls down, the volume in the chest cavity increases, causing a lower pressure inside the mouth relative to the air outside the body that surrounds the drink.)

The amount of time devoted to Extend should depend on how important the concept is to the discipline being taught, whether this idea will be revisited again in the days and weeks to come, and how strongly conveyed the student understanding was during the Explain phase.

Adaptations: This lesson can address numerous concepts (e.g., evaporative cooling, energy transfer, gas laws), so the teacher can, through guiding questions, focus conversations on specific content. For instance, if energy is the focus, then questions should help focus students on exploring and then explaining how energy is conserved during the motion of the Drinking Bird. As students discuss the properties of matter, they need to focus attention on the gas in the apparatus (closed system) and not the liquid (the volume of a gas is much more affected by temperature changes than the liquid).

Science Lesson 2: What Is Life?

Key Concepts: Cell structure; cell metabolism; energy transfer

Next Generation Science Standards: MS-LS1 From Molecules to Organisms; Structures and Processes; MS-LS2 Ecosystems: Interactions, Energy, and Dynamics; MS-LS3 Heredity: Inheritance and Variation of Traits

Objective: Students will compose and then defend a list of the characteristics that all living things need to possess.

Essential Question: What is necessary for life to exist?

Lesson Overview: As part of any life science course, students need to understand what defines life, how life is organized, and how the components of life interrelate. This investigation provides a solid introduction to cells and cell metabolism. Guiding questions for the lesson include "What is living, how do we know it is living, and why is this important?"

Engage: Students complete a card sort of 20 different pictures. In groups of two to three, have students sort each picture into one of three piles: living, nonliving, or uncertain. The pictures should include a variety of matter or organisms.

Teacher Support for Engage: The pictures can be modified for a younger audience or made more challenging for advanced students. Select pictures intentionally so that they range from the microscopic to the macroscopic, to encourage discussion. Some possible images are a robot, a computer, a chromosome, an animal, a pile of timber, a sugar cube, a DNA strand, an amoeba, aluminum, a red blood cell, fire, table salt, a virus, water, a heart, a flower, and an acorn.

Explore: After a brief discussion regarding what things they placed in each pile, students generate a concise list of the characteristics that all living things must possess. They should be prepared to defend their solution. Assess students informally in their groups as they create their list and discuss it with you while they work.

Teacher Support for Explore: The goal during the Explore phase is to get students thinking about and discussing the commonalities associated with those things that they are certain are living. As they begin making the list, they should be able to exclude those things placed in the nonliving pile as not fitting one or more of the items on their list. The goal is not for them to come up with a complete or perfect list. Rather, students need to use critical thinking to come up with a solid list that they can defend.

Explain: Groups each share one critical characteristic of living things from their list until all characteristics are listed on the board. Given a new card, groups should now be able to determine with confidence which pile it best associates with based on the list of characteristics. As a second portion of the Explain, give students a list of characteristics of living things that are commonly found in textbooks or used by researchers. Have students, in groups or individually, compare their list, the list on the board, and the provided list to create a final list that does not duplicate ideas. As a check for understanding, have each student briefly explain in his notebook why each characteristic is critical.

Teacher Support for Explain: For older students, provide a list that has some characteristics that are agreed on (e.g., "made of cells") and others that are not (e.g., "must have a neural network or brain"). This activity will allow them to filter through which characteristics are critical and which are not before they develop their final list.

Although the lists do not have to be the same, students need to realize that certain traits are critical (though they may be stated in different ways). All living things are made of cell(s), can reproduce (sexually or asexually), grow and develop, use and obtain energy, and respond to their environment. Clearly, many of the core ideas studied in a middle school or high school classroom are represented in this activity and discussion.

Extend: Have students justify why they think the following items are or are not living: peach pit, bacteria, tennis shoe, and nucleus of a cell. To check for understanding, students should list five living things, five nonliving things, and one thing that could be justified as either depending on how it is explained (none of their selected items may come from those discussed in class).

Teacher Support for Extend: The Extend activity requires students to continue to think about the world around them. Some students will likely be creative in coming up with a list of living and nonliving things, but, again, their defense of the items on the list is really the most important aspect. Some students will enjoy the discussions that spark controversy, such as whether viruses or red blood cells should be classified as living or nonliving.

Adaptations: Since biology is the study of life, it makes sense for students to investigate what distinguishes the living from nonliving in the world around them. Too often students think that anything discussed in biology is living. In a high school setting, this Explore lesson provides a transition to the study of biotic and abiotic factors in our environment.

At the elementary level, students study the characteristics of organisms. Students at this level might, as an Extend, defend their position on whether life could exist on other planets. Successful interactions would require that students make comparisons to what they already know about life on Earth.

Currently written for a middle school level, this lesson can easily be modified for high schoolers by focusing more on how the cells are organized and how the energy is used and regulated in the cells. This would occur as an Extend after students are first clear on the characteristics necessary for life to exist.

Science Lesson 3: The Atom as a Black Box

Key Concepts: Atomic structure; organization of matter; historical understanding of the atom

Next Generation Science Standard: MS-PS1/HS-PS1 Matter and Its Interactions

Objective: Students will investigate, question, and hypothesize the structure of the atom using prior knowledge, analogies, and tangible objects.

Essential Question: How can we understand what we cannot see?

Lesson Overview: Students often equate science to mystery—unexplainable, incomprehensible, and magical. This lesson confronts this "black box" image of science by asking students to investigate how we can understand that which we cannot directly see.

Engage: Begin by asking students to describe the smallest thing that can be seen by the human eye. Then have students list and describe the smallest things that they know exist even if they have not seen them. Have students provide any evidence that they have for knowing that these things really exist. Finally, ask them how someone could find out more about these things (assuming that money is no object).

Teacher Support for Engage: During the Engage phase, find out what students know regarding the atom and subatomic particles. Many students have heard or used terms like *atom* or *electron,* but these are abstract terms to students with little solid understanding. When pushed for how they know, most students will say because their 4th grade science teacher told them so. Leaving knowledge at such a shallow level without probing further only perpetuates the belief that science is magical and directly unknowable.

Explore: Pass sealed boxes around for students to investigate. Students may shake and sniff the box but not damage or open it. After using their senses, students should individually sketch their predictions of the contents and configuration inside the box. They should repeat the process for all four unique boxes.

Teacher Support for Explore: Jewelry boxes work well for this activity and are often cheaply acquired. Inside each box you should place a marble and an obstruction of some kind (duct taped or glued in place). See Figure 4.1 for some possible patterns for obstructions. I recommend constructing at least three boxes for each unique setup. Once boxes are constructed, seal them with duct tape around all edges, and label similar boxes with the same symbols (e.g., Xa, Bg, M—these should remind students of the periodic table but be different from an actual element symbol since they are not meant to model a specific atom).

Figure 4.1
Suggested Arrangement of Items in Boxes

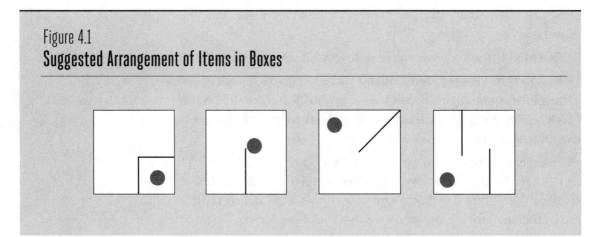

Explain: Have students in small groups discuss their predictions for what is inside each box along with their justification to support their answer. As a class, see if you can reach consensus on what each box looks like inside and what the justification was for reaching that conclusion. The boxes can then be used as an analogy to discuss the atom, which we also cannot directly see. Teacher questions should guide the Explain activity, beginning with the mystery boxes and ending with what we can and do know about the atom. For instance, the atom contains a dense, heavy nuclear core made up of protons and neutrons, with a spacious low-density outer region populated with electrons. The outermost electrons often interact with (share, donate, accept) electrons from other atoms.

Teacher Support for Explain: Students are not expected to discover the experiments that were conducted to determine the existence and relative proximities of the subatomic particles, but through the Explore phase, they can better understand the need for and contributions of each of these studies. The hope is to get students to understand that we can gather lots of other types of evidence about a system or phenomenon even if we are not able to sense it directly with our eyes.

The Explain is really two components: (1) processing the mystery boxes and (2) understanding our current view of atomic theory. The success of the Explain activity hinges largely on the ability to use the analogy of the mystery boxes to help students learn about the atom. In the first part of the Explain, your discussions should focus on how we know and how we are certain of what is inside the box instead of simply determining the correct pattern. At the culmination of the discussion, have an extra open box so that you can show the obstruction inside for one of the patterns. I would leave the others unopened, telling the students, "Often in science we do not know with absolute certainty what the actual answer is."

Extend: Students research in teams of two to three and then present their answer to one of many more advanced questions that you have posed, such as "Why do we typically limit our conversations and activities in chemistry classes to protons, neutrons, and electrons when there are many other subatomic particles—such as muons, gluons, leptons, quarks, and neutrinos, to name a few?"

Teacher Support for Extend: Although there are numerous other subatomic particles, protons, neutrons, and electrons are of primary concern for understanding how matter interacts at the basic level. Furthermore, electrons (the donating, accepting, or sharing particles), particularly in the outer valance shell, are essential to understanding ordinary chemical reactions. The protons and neutrons are secondary (though important). They are responsible for the majority of the mass of the atom or compound and play an important role in understanding nuclear chemistry. If considering other subatomic particles does not seem a valuable use of time, then devote more time to questioning and unpacking how and what we know about the atom and its interaction with other atoms.

Adaptations: This lesson gives students an opportunity to explore the seemingly hidden and mysterious world of the atom through the use of reasoning and analogies. It couples key content (atomic theory) with an investigation that addresses the nature of science. In the process, students gain scientific knowledge through critical thinking.

Although this lesson is designed primarily for high school physical science or chemistry classes, it would be equally appropriate for a middle school setting. Instead of aligning to atomic theory, the discussion could consider how phase changes occur.

Science Lesson 4: Where Has the Moon Gone?

Key Concepts: Relationship of the Earth-sun-moon system; relative movement of moon and sun relative to our position on Earth.

Next Generation Science Standard: MS-ESS1 Earth's Place in the Universe

Objective: Students will demonstrate through 3D physical models and 2D paper models how the various phases of the moon are created.

Essential Question: Where will the moon be at noon tomorrow? And noon the day after that?

Lesson Overview: Students have difficulty transferring a 2D model of the phases of the moon into what they see in the day and night sky. They also often have misconceptions regarding the moon and its movement relative to Earth. So students' misconceptions will be probed and then correct conceptions will be reinforced through exploration of the models and support from the explanation that follows.

Engage: Give a quick multiple-choice pretest to probe for common misconceptions. Questions should cover the relative size of the moon in relation to our sun, the relative distance of the moon from Earth, the length of a lunar day, the cause of a lunar eclipse, and the reason our moon is visible during the daylight hours at some times, yet only visible at night during other times.

Teacher Support for Engage: All students have observed the moon, but they typically have a large number of misconceptions about it. Once you uncover misconceptions, adjust the lesson so that it best allows students to explore these issues.

Explore: Given eight discs, each shaded to represent the key phases of the lunar cycle, students in teams of two to three organize the discs in the proper order on a lab counter, with Earth at the center of the counter. Then they are to place the cut out vocabulary words next to the corresponding disc: *new, full, waxing* (used twice), *waning* (used twice), *crescent* (used twice), *gibbous* (used twice), *first quarter,* and *third quarter.* Differentiated instruction is reinforced here because some students will be more confident in figuring out which vocabulary word fits with which image.

Teacher Support for Explore: Although students may have difficulty connecting all the vocabulary with the correct phase of the moon, most will get the phases in the correct order. The question that will puzzle many students will be whether the phases should be increasing in a clockwise or counterclockwise direction. (When viewed from the North Pole, the moon appears to move counterclockwise around Earth. If using a globe or daily observations to model this motion, students should begin by seeing that it appears to be moving to the east; then they can determine with a globe that this motion translates into counterclockwise when looking down from the North Pole.)

Explain: During the Explain phase, students will visually represent specific phases of the moon using 3D models (sun, Earth, moon). It is important that the model of Earth (a globe) has a dot for where the students are located. You can pause periodically and request that all students draw and explain how one or more phases of the moon are created.

Teacher Support for Explain: It will be clear by the end of the visual demonstrations that several misconceptions should be corrected and explicitly addressed. For instance, when modeling a phase of the moon, the sun must always be considerably farther from Earth than the moon (by a factor of nearly 400:1).

Extend: Have student groups research and then model one aspect of the Earth-sun-moon relationship. These topics may include solar versus annular eclipses, lunar eclipses, reasons for eclipses in some months but not others, the relative size of the three bodies, the relative distances of the three bodies, and the relationship of the period and rotation of our moon.

Teacher Support for Extend: Two-dimensional models are often helpful for simplicity, but they can be limiting. Specifically, it is challenging to explain how a new moon or full moon can be created without also creating, respectively, a solar (or at least annular) eclipse or a lunar eclipse every month. A 3D visual will show that the moon's orbit does not always fall in the same plane as the Earth-sun orbit. This Extend activity gives students an opportunity to become experts on one aspect associated with the interrelationship of the Earth-sun-moon, but it is critical in the process that all students understand each of the aspects. All students must know each topic or concept addressed relative to the moon.

Adaptations: The moon is a highly engaging topic, but it is also remarkably misunderstood. For instance, many students think the moon comes out only at night even though they have seen it during the day—which also tells us how difficult it is to alter a misconception once it has formed.

This lesson is written for a middle grade audience and standards but can easily be adapted for other audiences. At the elementary level, the lesson should focus on observing patterns associated with objects in our sky. Obviously, the moon and sun are the objects that are most visible and recognizable. The goal is to get students to explore the behavior of these objects in our sky. They could make maps of the sun's location at different times during the course of a day and at the same time each day. The same can be done with the moon except the timing needs to coincide with when it will be visible in the daytime sky. After collecting data for a couple of days, students of various ages can begin predicting where the moon or sun will be at a given time on the next day.

Sample Mathematics Lessons

The following sample math lessons are offered to show how you might facilitate an Explore-before-Explain inquiry-based lesson in your classroom.

Mathematics Lesson 1: Making Necklaces

Key Concept: Division of fractions

Common Core State Standard: Number System

Objective: Students will discover the reason behind the "invert and multiply" algorithm and will learn through exploration that division does not always make smaller.

Essential Question: How is the length of individual links related to the number of links needed to make a necklace of a particular length?

Lesson Overview: Students are asked to design and make 12-inch necklaces with links of various sizes made of construction paper. Through exploration, they will discover that dividing by a number less than 1 produces a result larger than the dividend as they invent an algorithm to divide fractions.

Engage: Pose questions about division in a short pretest: Can students model both measurement and partitive division contexts pictorially and symbolically? How does the value of the quotient compare to the dividend? Students should justify their response to the latter question; this step will reveal the extent of any misconceptions.

Teacher Support for Engage: An initial goal is to discover how well entrenched the misconception is that division makes numbers smaller. If your students believe this statement, then you can explicitly focus conversation on this misconception as each necklace is made. Another purpose of the Engage phase is to see whether students recognize the two different models for division. One is measurement division, which functions as repeated subtraction (as is the case in this investigation), and the other is partitive division (e.g., having 20 cards and determining how many cards each player would get when dealing the cards out to 4 players). If students cannot model problems with division, then offer several situations involving whole numbers before continuing.

Explore: Working in pairs, students make a set of 12-inch necklaces with fitting links. The links are of varying size: three inches, two inches, one inch, one-half inch, one-third inch, and one-fourth inch. Students must draw pictures of their necklaces and use mathematical operations to indicate how they would represent the number of links.

Teacher Support for Explore: Provide rulers, colored paper, and scissors so that students can measure and create the links they will use to make the necklaces. Monitor the discussion of the pairs, helping students recognize the repeated subtraction (measurement) context for division and ensuring that they understand that when the links are less than one inch, the number of links needed is greater than 12 (the number of inches for the total necklace). For each necklace, students should also draw a picture to scale, ensuring that their measures are reasonably accurate. For students new to fractions or who have solidly entrenched misconceptions, delay writing the problem in symbols until they are making sense of their models and pictures.

Explain: With guidance, students explain their results, showing their necklaces and pictures and indicating how they can represent the number of needed links using mathematical operations. During this discussion, ask students to reflect on the number of links needed and what this suggests about division.

Teacher Support for Explain: With unit fraction divisors, students should be able to demonstrate why the dividend is multiplied by the reciprocal of the unit link. Although they have not yet had the experiences needed for the traditional algorithm, this is a key component that the students must be able to explain as a result of their experiences building the necklaces. They should also confront directly the idea that division by a number less than 1 produces a quotient larger than the dividend.

Extend: Ask students questions related to different contexts involving division by unit fractions (e.g., "How many people can be served with six pizzas if each person eats one-eighth of a pizza?"). Link prior ideas by asking how the quotient can be larger than the dividend, and reference the pretest; then return to the necklace problem. Again, students are to make 12-inch necklaces, but this time the sets of links are one-third and two-thirds inches; one-fourth, two-fourths, and three-fourths inches; and one-sixth, two-sixths, three-sixths, four-sixths, and five-sixths inches. As before, students create the necklaces, draw them, and represent the number of needed links with mathematical operations, searching for patterns in the numbers.

Teacher Support for Extend: To extend the ideas learned, students embark on another Explore-Explain sequence. They discover and then internalize, for example, that there are exactly half as many links when each link is two-thirds inch compared to when the links are one-third inch. After students have created the necklaces, drawn pictures, and recognized the relationship between the numerator (as well as the denominator) of the divisor and the final quotient, lead students to the standard algorithm for dividing fractions and provide sufficient time for students to practice using the algorithm.

Adaptations: Keep the problem concrete for students who are new to or struggle with fractions. Specifically, you can use physical models and drawings of the models in several situations before using symbols to represent (not perform) the division that is occurring. Students must have sufficient experiences as they progress from the concrete to the pictorial to the abstraction of the symbols.

You can, through questioning, modify the numbers—using less common fractions, changing the dividend to a mixed number, altering the problem so that the links don't fit perfectly—and then alter the problem so that the necklace length is less than 1 link (thus making it a partial necklace). These adaptations provide an excellent opportunity for differentiated learning. One way to include some of these adaptations is to change the units from inches to feet, which helps students have a clearer understanding of the importance of units and how we can work with them.

Mathematics Lesson 2: Easy Access

Key Concepts: Rate of change; slope; Pythagorean theorem

Common Core State Standards: Expressions and Equations (middle school); Algebra (high school); Geometry

Objective: Students will design a wheelchair ramp as they develop ideas about slope and use the Pythagorean theorem. An alternative objective to hook student interest is to ask them to design a skateboard ramp or a ski jump.

Essential Question: How steep should a ramp be to allow wheelchair access?

Lesson Overview: Through measurement, students design a ramp that can be used instead of steps at the front of the school building (or another set of steps). Through research, students determine how steep they can build the ramp so that people in wheelchairs can use it.

Engage: Challenge students to design a ramp that provides wheelchair access in place of a stairway. Ask students what information they will need and how they might go about the design. This questioning helps you determine what students know about rate of change.

Teacher Support for Engage: Elicit prior knowledge that students have about slope, both in the general sense and in the specific, procedural sense. Students may have an intuitive understanding of what a steep slope means and even what a positive, negative, or zero slope means. After presenting the challenge, monitor the students to determine if they are asking appropriate questions, such as how many steps there are, how high each step is, and how deep each step is. If necessary, prompt them with leading questions. Before continuing, confirm that students are adept at measuring—or have some proficiency with rulers, measuring tapes, and units. Determine if your students need a short lesson on measuring before proceeding.

Explore: Working in groups of two or three, students design the ramp. Be prepared to give students needed measuring tools upon request. Monitor groups to ensure that they realize they need to know how many steps there are, how much vertical distance they need, and how much horizontal distance they need. Encourage students, as they work, to determine whether it would be realistic for a wheelchair to make it up and down the ramp. What considerations are important?

Teacher Support for Explore: Some leading questions may be needed (e.g., "How do you know how much horizontal and vertical distance is needed to support the ramp?") to assess whether students recognize the information they need. Students must document their results with numbers, pictures, and graphs and be prepared to share their results. For groups that proceed more quickly, ask questions about the length and angle of the ramp itself (and not just the vertical and horizontal requirements). Students also investigate how steep wheelchair ramps can be. Are there legal restrictions? Are there practical restrictions? According to the New Disability website (www.newdisability.com/wheelchairramp. htm), the steepest is a ratio of 1 unit of rise to 12 units of run, and less steep is preferable. What would students have to do to ensure that they are designing a useable ramp? They also might investigate the materials, consider durability and stability, as well as determine the need for landing areas and switchbacks.

Explain: With guidance, students explain their results, presenting them numerically and graphically. As groups present, check to be sure that students understand how to determine the length of the ramp and how much rise and run are needed, which leads to discussing the term *slope* and its definition.

Teacher Support for Explain: The underlying mathematical ideas, including the appropriate vocabulary, will be teased out during the Explain phase. Students should present their findings orally. As they do so, introduce the concept of slope and ask students about the ratio of rise to run: "If something is steeper, does that suggest rise:run or run:rise is larger? Why?" By comparing different groups' designs, you can guide students from their intuitive understanding to a reasonably deep understanding of slope. Initially, avoid considerations of positive versus negative slopes. Instead, focus students on how steep or how shallow something like the ramp rises and how we quantify this measurement. Students may be surprised at how shallow a wheelchair-accessible ramp must be unless they're able to walk on one and experience it. Even better, borrow a wheelchair and have them test a ramp (only if safe, of course). Within the explanation, a discussion of what a slope of one-half, 1, or 2 looks like helps students begin to have a sense of slope from their previous experience and ways we quantify it.

Extend: Next, suggest a context that moves away from physical slope. For instance, ask students to pretend they have $120 saved and deplete it at the rate of $8 per week. Students identify and explore the relationship between the variables, representing the relationship in different ways and determining how this problem is similar to the initial problem of building steps. This discussion further develops the idea of slope as the ratio of change of the dependent variable to the change in the independent variable.

Teacher Support for Extend: After assessing students' mastery of the wheelchair ramp, extend the concept of slope to a situation in which slope is not manifested physically. Of course, the slope remains the ratio of the vertical change to the horizontal change, or the ratio of the change in the dependent variable to the change in the independent variable. How much does our dependent variable change as we alter our independent variable by one unit? By two units?

Situations involving arithmetic sequences present an excellent opportunity to examine this concept. Students investigate the scenario of having savings of $120 that is being depleted at a rate of $8 per week. After they identify the independent variable as time (weeks elapsed) and the dependent variable as money (dollars remaining), they can create a table of values and then graph the table. As they study both the table and the graph, ask them questions such as "How does the amount of money remaining change as each week passes?" and "For every two weeks that pass, how does the amount of money remaining change?" Ask students to show their answers on the table and on the graph. This activity helps you assess whether students recognize that the slope is negative and constant, and that the ratio of the amount of money remaining to the amount of time that has elapsed is constant no matter which points they select. This scenario is an opportunity not only to help students further develop their understanding of slope but to develop other important ideas, including x- and y-intercepts, domain and range, increasing and decreasing functions, and the fact that linear functions have constant slope.

Adaptations: As with any inquiry lesson, you should prepare several questions ahead of time that challenge groups of students at the appropriate level. This lesson can help students connect measurement, the Pythagorean theorem, and an understanding of slope as rate of change, but you may ignore the Pythagorean theorem if it will distract from the main purpose of the lesson—developing an intuitive understanding of slope. More advanced students can design transitions in their ramps and determine the materials and costs of building a ramp that can realistically service wheelchairs.

Mathematics Lesson 3: Where Should We Meet?

Key Concepts: Characteristics of median; organizing data

Common Core State Standards: Statistics and Probability

Objective: Students will discover through exploration that the median is the measure of center that minimizes the distance to all points in a data set.

Essential Question: What location minimizes the total distance traveled for a group traveling from various distances?

Lesson Overview: Students are asked to determine where a group of five people, all positioned along the same highway, should meet in order to minimize the total distance traveled. Through discovery, they determine that the median serves this purpose. They then extend their finding to a set of six numbers and then to any data set.

Engage: Pose the following problem: Five police officers who need to meet are on the same highway, at mile markers 2, 4, 16, 28, and 50. Where should they meet to minimize the total distance traveled? Students must write down what they think, giving you an opportunity to check for prior understanding or misconceptions and to determine whether students guess or use previously studied ideas of measure of center.

Teacher Support for Engage: By asking students to make a prediction prior to exploring the problem, you can determine whether students use a measure of center (possibly the mean), consider only the smallest and largest values, or guess randomly. This discussion helps identify whether students have misconceptions, which can be confronted later, or whether they have no justification at all for their response.

Explore: As students work in groups of two or three, assess the strategy that students use for solving the problem. Challenge those who solve the problem more quickly to create their own set of five values and solve the problem. All students are challenged to determine the answer given any set of five numbers, discovering that the median is the value that minimizes the distance.

Teacher Support for Explore: A major part of Explore requires students to determine how they might best approach the problem. The results of this assessment may tell you that some students need prompting to determine the total number of miles driven to a specific location. Other students may need some guiding questions to help organize their data to assist in looking for patterns. Students, however, should be able to guide most of the exploration with a minimum of teacher intervention.

Explain: Students present and explain their findings. With guidance, students find that as they move in either direction away from the median, while they get closer to two points, they get farther from three points, thus increasing the distance. Assess whether students make the argument if there are three values, seven values, nine values, or any odd number of values. Through the explanation and demonstration of why this is the case, students learn that, at least for a data set with an odd number of values, the median, not the mean, minimizes the distance to the points.

Teacher Support for Explain: Once students have realized that the minimal distance is reached at mile marker 16, focus on the justification as to why this is the case. Again with prompting questions, students should recognize 16 as the middle, or median, value of the data set and that for any set of five values, the minimum distance is achieved at the median. By asking students as they move toward or away from the median how many points they're getting closer to and how many they are getting farther away from, you can assess whether students understand and can explain in writing why, if they start at the median and move away from it, the total distance must necessarily increase. Thus, the median is the optimal value.

Extend: Add a sixth point at mile marker 80. Though some students may think they know the answer right away, most will be in for a surprise as they explore what happens with an even number of data points. This second exploration leads to a second explanation, in which the students should play a prominent role.

Teacher Support for Extend: Once students understand that the median minimizes the total distance to all values for an odd-number data set, they explore what happens with an even number of data points. Using the same logic as before, they discover that any point between the two middle-most points, including those points, works. So why do we consider the median to be the midpoint of the two points closest to the middle? Students should see that it is simply a matter of convenience to identify a single value. More advanced students may extend their exploration and explanations into the distinction between continuous and discrete data sets, concepts that have an impact on the interpretation of the median.

Adaptations: Be prepared to help the students create a graphical model and encourage them to organize their data systematically. You should also assess whether students can convince others that their solution is correct. For struggling students, you might suggest that they create a number line. By asking probing questions, you can guide explorations so that the discussion includes absolute value (the sum of distances for all potential solutions) or integers (systematically comparing one value with an adjacent value to determine whether they are getting closer or farther from the various points). To provide greater challenge, include integers, rational numbers, and real numbers instead of just whole numbers.

Mathematics Lesson 4: The Family of Polynomial Functions

Key Concepts: Roots; end behavior; finite differences of polynomial functions

Common Core State Standards: Algebra

Objectives: Using graphing calculators, students will discover the number of complex and possible real roots of polynomial functions and determine how to predict the end behavior by knowing the degree and leading coefficient. They will also investigate the relationship between the degree of the polynomial and the finite differences of the polynomial, laying the foundation for the future study of calculus.

Essential Question: How does the degree of a polynomial function affect the number of roots, its end behavior, and the finite differences between consecutive values?

Lesson Overview: Using graphing calculators, students create polynomial functions of degrees 2, 3, 4, and 5; explore the number of real and complex roots, end behavior, and the finite differences. They then formulate conjectures that generate insights into polynomials and into the derivatives of polynomials, a topic they will study in the future.

Engage: Using a short pretest, gather information about students' prior knowledge of polynomials, including the number of complex and real roots, the end behavior of the functions, and the finite differences for polynomials of different degrees.

Teacher Support for Engage: For students who have been previously taught procedurally, you will likely find some teaching and reteaching necessary before moving on to the Explore section. For example, you may have to provide more leading questions, such as "What is the value of the polynomial when x is 10, 100, or 1,000?" to guide students into an understanding of end behavior and how they can predict it from looking at a polynomial. Students may need help using technology to populate tables of values quickly and efficiently and to adjust views so that they can see the components of a graph.

Explore: Working in small groups, students create several polynomials of degree 2, 3, 4, and 5. Using graphing calculators, they explore the number of real and complex roots; the end behavior; and the first-, second-, third-, and fourth-order finite differences.

Teacher Support for Explore: Remediation may be necessary to lead students to understand the connection between graphs and the algebraic solution of roots. Through exploration, students discover that the highest-degree term has by far the largest effect on a polynomial for very large (in both a positive and negative sense) values of the independent variable. Demonstrate how to find the finite differences for a set of values (something that certain graphing calculators can produce easily), assuming the independent variable is arranged in an arithmetic sequence. You should, through observation, be constantly assessing how well the students are doing as they look for patterns among the degree, the coefficient of the leading term, and the end behavior; and the relationship between the degree and the finite differences.

Explain: Students present their findings, moving from degree 2 to degree 5, while you assess for understanding. They should have discovered that a polynomial of degree N has N complex roots and up to N real roots, that odd degrees have opposite end behavior (± infinity), that even degrees have similar end behavior (either + or – infinity), and that the Nth order finite differences are constant. Additionally, they should find that first-order differences are degree $N-1$, second-order differences are $N-2$, and so on.

Teacher Support for Explain: Assess whether students form their conjectures too quickly or if they waited until analyzing several examples. Reasons behind the end behavior and the number of real roots should come fairly readily, but students may need many examples to grasp why the first-order differences for linear functions are constant and why the second-order differences for quadratic functions are constant. You should guide the discourse so that there is a good mix of numerical and graphical representations, which some graphing calculator models can facilitate. Contextual problems (e.g., "How many games must be played if a league has eight teams and each team plays the others one time?") that can be solved numerically, algebraically, and geometrically may help solidify the ideas. Once you are assured that students understand how linear and quadratic functions change, then you can move on to higher-order polynomials.

Extend: Give students a constant value that represents, say, the third-order differences. Have students try to rebuild the original polynomial as they deepen their knowledge of how polynomial functions work.

Teacher Support for Extend: Just as exploring finite differences sows the seeds for the understanding of derivatives, reversing the process sows the seeds for integration. The starting value is analogous to the constant that is added to indefinite integrals. By building the function first numerically, then graphically, and then algebraically, students will gain some deep insights into the nature of polynomial functions, and these insights will help prepare them for future study in mathematics.

Adaptations: You should be alert to students' prior understanding of functions, roots, and end behavior. If students have not worked from a table of values to a function, you should be prepared to remediate. Rather than asking students to create their own polynomials, provide the polynomials and guide students through the exploration and analysis of the roots, end behavior, and finite differences. Certain graphing calculators cannot find complex roots; in this case, you should restrict the investigation to quadratics, cubics with one rational root, and quartics that are readily factorable or have two easily determined rational roots.

Some calculators do not have a feature that quickly determines the finite differences; in this case, students can, on their own, perform the subtraction between successive values in the dependent variable. To keep the number of computations manageable, you can limit the number of values used for the independent variable to six or seven.

Finally, regardless of the calculator model being used, instead of leaving students to their own devices for the Extend phase, you can guide students through rebuilding the polynomial, providing a starting point (the constant added when integrating in calculus). The students can also use regression on their calculators to rebuild the functions as they determine specific values that need to be included.

Being intentional about the curriculum, assessments, discourse, and instruction are four critical aspects associated with effective teaching. This chapter has illustrated eight unique examples of how the 4E x 2 Instructional Model can be used to lead effective standards-based, inquiry-based instruction. The specific examples provided may fit well into your instructional sequence and can thus be taken, adapted for your needs, and used with your students. However, the examples should also provide insights into what effective lessons look like so that you or teams of teachers at your school can begin to construct inquiry-based lessons that best meet the needs of your students and the standards that you seek to address. One goal may be to add one solidly constructed inquiry-based lesson each nine weeks. That timeline should give you time to plan, implement, and then evaluate the success of the lesson. It will become exponentially easier and quicker to plan each ensuing lesson, so don't become discouraged if the first lesson takes considerable time to plan well. The next chapter will detail how an inquiry lesson sequence can be developed into a unit of study around a core idea such as energy or probability.

5

How Do Inquiry and Core Ideas Appear in Units of Study?

As educators, we often lose sight of the forest for all the trees. What a student needs to know at the end of the course is often blurred as we become too deeply focused on the day-to-day minutiae of making sure we have enough graded work for the term, keeping students busy, and ensuring students are compliant. Being intentional about one's instructional practice means continually referring to the core ideas that you want students to know and be able to do by the end of the school year.

In the last chapter, we looked at guided inquiry lessons lasting a day or two of instruction that incorporated a major concept. Typically spanning a week or more, the lessons in this chapter emphasize a core idea for the discipline that is central to the entire year of learning. We will look at two instructional units, one on science and one on mathematics.

Science Unit

Mousetrap Racers focuses on the major ideas of force, motion, and transfer of energy. Even though the unit is directed toward learning science, it clearly ties to mathematics, technology, and engineering. The unit does not attempt to incorporate all the lessons that you would likely use to teach these topics, but it does provide a solid framework that allows for references to the learning in this unit throughout the year.

Mousetrap Racers: Middle-Grades Study of Force, Motion, and Energy

Key Concepts: Time, distance, speed, and acceleration relationships; Newton's Laws of Motion; mechanical, kinetic, and potential energy relationships

Next Generation Science Standards: MS-PS2 Motion and Stability: Forces and Interactions; MS-PS3 Energy

Objective: Students will design, create, test, and then explore the concepts of force and motion as they measure the performance of their mousetrap vehicles.

Essential Question: What factors affect the motion of an object?

Unit Overview: Students create a mousetrap vehicle that travels five meters as fast as possible without going over six meters. The unit sequence is Engage 1 (check for misconceptions) → Engage 2 (discuss motion) → Explore 1 (pose challenge) → Explain 1 (discuss design) → Explore 2 (construct vehicle) → Explain 2 (discuss construction) → Explore 3 (test vehicle and collect data) → Explain 3 (analyze and communicate findings) → Extend 1 (explore new scenario).

Engage 1: Begin with a pretest of common misconceptions related to motion, forces, and energy to gauge prior knowledge. The pretest should be quick but also effectively sample your objectives. Your quiz might include true/false items:

1. If speed increases, then the object is accelerating.

2. All moving objects will stop if there is no friction.

3. If something is in motion, then a force must be acting on it.

4. Objects at rest have no forces acting on them.

5. When an object travels twice as fast, it has twice as much energy.

6. Potential energy (stored energy) is not really energy until it is released.

7. If an object is stationary, then it does not have any energy.

8. Heat is a substance and not a form of energy.

9. If designed well, a machine should not lose usable energy.

10. Energy cannot change forms (e.g., once kinetic, always kinetic).

Each of these items is false and addresses a common misconception held by students, but you may want to restate some of the items so that you have both true and false statements. The pretest is about gathering meaningful data for you as an instructor—not providing correct answers at this time. You should make time to revisit each item at the end of the unit and see if your students' responses have changed.

Engage 2: Show your class several photos or images of cars, boats, trains, and planes in various states of motion. Ask students to describe the motion of the object found in each image. After discussing motion with students, develop a KWHL chart (described in Chapter 3) as a class that represents what students already know about factors affecting the motion of vehicles and any questions they have. A disadvantage to constructing the KWHL chart as a class, however, is that you might miss individual students' misconceptions. I would recommend, therefore, that you ask students to jot down their own questions in their science notebooks.

Teacher Support for Engage 1: As students call out adjectives involving the motion of the objects (*fast, slow,* etc.), ask students to compare the vehicles: "What causes the object(s) to move? Which vehicle would be the fastest? Slowest?" Try to avoid using terms such as *speed, velocity, direction, force, friction,* and *acceleration*—let those words come from students (if they are used at all) to see how they use them in context. You will probably discover some misconceptions. Ask students to provide possible reasons for these differences in speed: "What do the fastest vehicles have in common? What do the slowest vehicles have in common?" Watch for misconceptions such as using *acceleration* and *speed* interchangeably.

Here's where the H (for *how*) in the KWHL chart is vital because it encourages students to ask scientific questions and then seek solutions to those questions. To make this point more explicit, have students brainstorm several scientific questions that could be studied in relation to motion of vehicles. This activity will allow them to work with independent and dependent variables and develop strong scientific questions that are testable. Students can record these responses in their science notebooks and then share them with the class. KWHL charts can be done individually, in groups, or with the entire class. The advantage of creating one as a whole class now is that the students' ideas can be revisited during the lesson and at the end of the lesson as the L portion is completed.

Explore 1: Pose the following challenge to your students: create a mousetrap vehicle that travels five meters as fast as possible without going over six meters. In teams of two or three students, guide your class through the planning phase. Give teams the vehicle parts and have them discuss how they will create such a vehicle. Allow 15 to 20 minutes for teams to develop a vehicle design, as well as an explanation of how it will achieve the goal. Students can begin assembling their vehicle only after you have approved their design.

Teacher Support for Explore 1: The actual parameters of this assignment are not as critical as finding a way to challenge students to work with the key concepts. Students often get lost in the challenge itself, so it is important to pause often to discuss the science involved (e.g., "What happens to the motion of the vehicle as the length of the throw arm on the mouse trap increases?"). This Explore activity provides an excellent opportunity to incorporate science, technology, engineering, and mathematics.

Feel free to modify the constraints and rules, as you deem appropriate. I chose to include speed (fastest to five meters) and the ability to stop (not to exceed six meters) because many kits and contests focus solely on speed, but my variation integrates the following concepts into learning: force, friction, energy transformation, speed, acceleration, and deceleration. Being intentional requires that you align the challenge with the students' ability levels so that they do not become overly frustrated while being cognizant of the concepts and objectives being taught.

As noted, I recommend not allowing students to begin construction until you have approved their plan. This step ensures that safety issues have been checked, and it gives you an opportunity to redirect and question students if they are heading down a path that will not lead to at least partial success (e.g., gluing the axle directly to the chassis of the car will not allow the wheels to turn).

Although most store-bought mousetrap racers come with directions, I prefer to encourage students to create their design without offering instructions. If they become frustrated, you can always offer some tips. The planning phase will likely bring up all sorts of questions, such as "How do we get it to roll?" and "How do we get it to move five meters but not six?" These questions do not occur if you provide one set of directions to everyone at the beginning. You will invariably have whole-class or small-group discussions to consider topics such as how to assemble the vehicle and what provides the force to make it vehicle move. The only component of this challenge that should be consistent and that should make it fair for everyone is using the same power source (i.e., a mousetrap).

Explain 1: After students have designed their vehicles, allow a few minutes for students to share ideas with other teams and discuss any challenges that they still have. The class as a whole could also discuss general approaches, realizations, and concerns before the actual construction ensues.

Teacher Support for Explain 1: Although discussion with other groups and as a class should be encouraged, many students will not be able to foresee and then address issues with the design until they actually construct the vehicle. To encourage success without simply giving steps to follow, consider asking the following questions, pausing a minute or two after each one so that the teams can discuss a response: (1) How will you get the vehicle to move? (2) How will you get it to move at least five meters? (3) How will you get it to stop before six meters? (4) What will help to ensure that your vehicle is reliable? (5) What is the greatest weakness of your design, and how can you improve it?

Explore 2: Students construct their mousetrap racers. A class discussion midway through the construction phase may help resolve any problems.

Teacher Support for Explore 2: The greatest safety issues for this lesson include the use of hot glue guns, cutting tools (e.g., often utility knives with a razor blade), drills, and the mousetrap spring. Discuss precautions regarding the hot glue guns before starting. You may need to stand by the gluing station. Make sure that you have a hot mat to catch excess glue so that counters are not damaged. Also make sure that students use a cutting mat with the knives and that all knives and tools are accounted for before dismissing class. Illustrate the power of the mousetrap with a small piece of wood, and demonstrate how the traps are properly used and set. Do not allow any trap larger than a mousetrap to be used. Make sure that designs are feasible before students begin cutting or gluing parts. Have scrap pieces available, as mistakes will occur. Also, supply extra pieces that students may want to incorporate into their vehicles to encourage creativity. You can test any parts ahead of time to see if you need to predrill or widen any predrilled holes so that they fit appropriately (e.g., sometimes the wheels do not fit the axle well and need to be drilled).

Explain 2: Before testing vehicles, discuss any issues regarding the successful construction of the vehicle (some groups may not have completed construction yet because of unforeseen complications) and how students will test and gather data on their vehicle.

Teacher Support for Explain 2: Challenge students to determine both the speed and acceleration of their vehicles if possible (even if the vehicle lacks the ability to travel the full distance). For younger students, you may need to guide them in how to calculate speed and acceleration. Specifically, they only need two points, (0 seconds, 0 meters) and (final time, final distance), to determine average speed, but they will need at least three points to determine whether the vehicle was accelerating. So, teams may have to work together to gather the data needed for acceleration. Some students may be interested in determining which vehicle in the class is fastest off the starting line (i.e., fastest initial acceleration) and which vehicle is fastest to the finish line (fastest overall average speed or continual acceleration)—and these vehicles may not necessarily be the same.

Explore 3: After cars have all been assembled, students should (1) test the performance of their vehicle, (2) gather and analyze the data, and (3) communicate findings and understanding.

Teacher Support for Explore 3: Students will need stopwatches (or potentially features on their cell phones), measuring tapes, and a long flat surface for testing the cars. Before data collection occurs, students need to ask a scientific question to guide their investigation. Either individual teams or the entire class could determine the scientific question to be studied. The questions should tie into the class objectives, so if your objective is that students will create and interpret distance and time graphs, then the question needs to align with this objective. Exploring rich scientific questions that are aligned to the topic being explored provides students with great practice in working with controls and independent and dependent variables.

Generally, students will record their initial trial times and then work on making modifications to the car in order to increase its speed and performance. So, an appropriate research question would be to determine how the performance of the vehicle improves as each modification is made. Students should represent their data for the initial trial as well as any follow-up runs after making modifications, and then they should reflect on their experiences in their science notebooks. While the design and construction are important, the most important math and science concepts can be explored during the vehicle-testing phase, and this is where teacher facilitation plays an important role. Have students control for a variable and graph the performance of their vehicles relative to each situation (e.g., using different tires, changing the length of the lever, or changing the gearing on the car).

Explain 3: The prior two Explain activities allowed for formative checks to assess student progress in terms of their vehicles' design and construction. Explain 3 explicitly ties these ideas together.

Teacher Support for Explain 3: After initial testing and data collection, bring all students back together for a group discussion, asking them, "What surprised you during the investigation? What did you discover about the motion of your car? What did you change about your car to improve its performance?" Then shift the discussion to communicating the students' data in effective ways. Questions might include "How would you share your results with others? How can you best represent your data visually?" Have students create group presentations to discuss, for example, data from their initial trials compared with data after they made some modifications. Whatever is communicated needs to be directly tied to the scientific questions being investigated by the group or the class.

Explain 3 is a good place to review and clarify important vocabulary that students use during their presentations (e.g., *distance, speed, acceleration, force, friction*). Important questions during presentations should center on the data collected and the visuals (graphs) created. For instance, in a graph of distance versus time, students will see that one line is steeper than the other. They need to understand (not just be told) that the one that was steeper was faster—assuming the coordinates and scaling are the same on both graphs. They do not need the concept of slope, but this activity will introduce them to the idea that the line has an important meaning that can be interpreted.

Another option is for students to compare their results and modifications with those of other teams in small-group settings. Students can then reflect in their science notebooks on what influences a vehicle's performance. Graphs and data should be compared among groups to see how well students really understand what they have demonstrated in their graphs.

With group projects, the majority of points earned should come from individual accountability. You can verify accountability in many ways, but reviewing science notebooks is a good option. Also, be sure that creativity, vehicle performance, and participation are not the majority of credit earned. Credit should be focused on content-related issues. At the end of team projects, students need a way to individually show their knowledge on the project and related concepts—through guided individual summaries, quizzes that test the concepts that were discussed, or a clear ability to verbally communicate their ideas.

Extend 1: Depending on students' mastery of conceptual development, the Extend phase can take many different paths. These paths need not be the same for all students, so you can easily offer differentiated instruction during this phase.

Option 1: After the presentations, suggest additional scenarios related to the motion of the cars; for example, "What would happen if you tested the cars on a different surface? What if the tires were made from a different material or had a different radius?"

Option 2: To emphasize the concept of force, ask students to redesign the car for steeper terrain. You may want to provide an additional energy source such as a rubber band to help the cars achieve steeper inclines. This activity will bring up issues around force, gearing, and other topics where students can continue to gather and analyze data. To achieve this feat, students will have to consider levers, gearing, springs, and simple machines.

Option 3: You might create task cards that describe the specifications for the vehicle. For example, one group may have the task of designing a vehicle to travel in a mountainous terrain, and another group may be given the task of designing a race car. Students work in groups to sketch the vehicle and describe the components of the design that will fit the specifications. The groups may also develop a marketing plan for their car, if time allows.

Teacher Support for Extend 1: Any assessments in the Extend phase should focus on making sure students have mastered the concepts, which requires them to apply this knowledge to new situations, and include a mix of practical, concrete applications and more traditional forms of assessment.

Adaptations: Students enjoy an engaging means to study motion, force, and energy through the mousetrap racer unit. However, you can increase the odds for success by adapting the unit to ability levels, course objectives, and resources available. For example, if you do not have the funds to purchase mousetrap racer kits, then several options are available: (1) purchase several mousetraps and then allow students to bring in scrap materials that don't exceed $1 in total cost, (2) use pull-and-release toy cars that move because of stored mechanical energy (i.e., internal spring), or (3) use the students' own Matchbox cars with a ramp or rubber band to supply the needed force to move the object.

If your students have limited exposure to inquiry-based learning, then they may need scaffolding. However, instead of simply providing instructions, lead a class discussion in which students examine collectively how to get the vehicle to move quickly, stop quickly, and be reliable. For classes that need more guidance, you may want to reconvene as a class between the planning, construction, and testing phases to discuss critical issues, clarify goals, and check for progress.

For the Engage 2 activity—and likely only for high school students—a second option would be to give students the following scenario: "The local sheriff's office needs your help to find out whether speeding is an issue on the stretch of road in front of the school. You will report your findings to the city council, which must decide if more traffic officers are needed."

This activity could also be done as an Extend at the end of the lesson, or as a performance assessment to determine the level of mastery acquired. Provide students with calculators, stopwatches, graph paper, and two meters of string. Because students may be working near a busy road, also review safety precautions with them beforehand. After some discussion, the students should be able to determine how to collect the data and then determine the speed. Specifically, they could measure the time it takes for passing cars to travel a premeasured distance (e.g., 10 meters, 25 meters). A straightforward calculation of $s = d/t$ provides the speed in meters/second, which they must convert to miles/hour before they can answer the initial question posed in the challenge. This brings up an important question about how much information is necessary: should students collect data for 1, 5, or 20 cars? Also, if students mingle too close to the road, drivers will likely slow down, thus influencing the results of the study.

Mathematics Unit

This unit focuses on statistical literacy in the middle grades. Every day, we are inundated with data, graphs, and arguments that affect our lives and society, yet most adults never reach minimum competence in this important area of mathematics. Despite its importance and its value in developing students' number sense (e.g., fractions, decimals, and percentages), the study of statistics is usually relegated to a superficial lesson or two on calculating the mean, median, and mode. Too often in mathematics, little attention is paid to the nature of variables, such as whether a problem is univariate or bivariate or whether the variable is categorical or numerical; statistics again provides a context for this type of analysis. In short, statistics can serve as a thread to tie the study of mathematics together. After all, if we are unable to make sense of a set of data, what is our purpose in studying mathematics at all?

Statistically Speaking: Middle-Grades Study of Statistical Literacy

The dynamic nature of the 4E × 2 Instructional Model allows considerable flexibility. The science unit was a series of related Explore and Explain sequences, but this math unit is framed by four discrete inquiry-based lessons that collectively work to build students' statistical literacy. These math lessons include studying the probabilistic nature of common events, developing strategies for describing and representing data, investigating important characteristics of measures of center, and exploring measures of dispersion (spread). Though not all-inclusive, this unit does capture many of the big ideas expressed in the Common Core State Standards for statistical literacy at the middle-grades level. I assume students have had an introduction to measures of center (specifically, mean, median, and mode), basic statistical graphs (including pie charts, boxplots, and histograms), and the basics of probability.

Unit Overview: The unit begins with a simulation to help students learn how to gather, organize, and interpret data as they make connections between relative frequencies and probabilities. Next, two problems are designed to help students master key characteristics of the mean and median. The unit concludes with an investigation in which students explore the effects of two different transformations on measures of center and measures of spread.

Mathematics Lesson 1: Are You Lucky?

Key Concepts: Simulations; organizing, representing, and interpreting data

Common Core State Standards: Investigate chance processes and develop, use, and evaluate probability models. Approximate the probability of a chance event by collecting data.

Objectives: Students will design and carry out a simulation of a binomial situation, organize their data, analyze them, and interpret their results.

Essential Question: What is the probability that when you guess blindly on four true/false questions, you will get at least three correct answers?

Lesson Overview: Working in small groups, students will design a simulation to determine the probabilities of getting zero, one, two, three, or all four answers correct when they guess on a true/false test. Students then extend their thinking to other contexts for which the mathematical strategies and ideas are similar.

Engage/Present the following scenario: A student takes a social studies test and guesses blindly on four true/false items. How many questions can the student expect to answer correctly, and what are the chances of getting at least three of the questions right?

Teacher Support for Engage: Based on responses, determine if students understand that the expected value is 2. Ask groups what the chances are of getting at least three correct answers. The Engage phase of the lesson seeks to find out students' prior knowledge but also misconceptions about probability.

Explore: In groups of two or three, students design a simulation using coins, spinners, number cubes, or a random number generator on a calculator. They conduct at least 50 trials and determine how to report the data, analyze the results, and communicate their method, results, and analysis to their peers.

Teacher Support for Explore: During the Explore, ensure that students are determining how many questions were answered correctly, not how many were true and how many were false. You may need to help students understand that they really are not interested in the specific answer, but whether the guess was correct or not. Some students may struggle with how to use a number cube or spinner to simulate the context, whereas more advanced students can be challenged with a question such as "How could you use a spinner that has five equal areas to conduct the simulation?"

Students should also develop a strategy for keeping track of their raw data and then figure out a way to represent and summarize their results. They should be able to create a frequency table, a relative frequency table, and a histogram for their results. Depending on your students' background, you may ask the class to determine summary statistics, including mean, median, and mode, and possibly the quartiles.

Explain: With guidance, students explain their simulation strategies. Ensure that students' strategies are justified based on the results and analysis of their tables or graphs. Students must then determine the probabilities, based on their results, of obtaining zero, one, two, three, or four correct responses; then they compare their results with their initial estimates. Depending on time, each group can present results either to the entire class or to two other groups. Challenge students with questions such as "What is the probability of getting at least three correct answers?"

Teacher Support for Explain: During presentations, students should explain why their strategy for the simulation is sound and what they found. Groups should compare their results with other groups' results, which will lead to a discussion about variability, as the groups' results, though probably reasonably similar, will not be exactly the same. The discussion should also include mention of the need for as many trials as possible, something that can be done efficiently with technology. (Various websites are available to conduct, say, 1,000 trials in short order. For one such website, see www.random.org.)

Encourage students to ask questions of each other: "Why did you record your results this way? What does your graph tell you?" Also help them make the connection between their results and the probability of getting a certain number of correct answers. Questions such as the following can help: "What is the probability of getting at least two of the four correct? How does what happened help you answer this for the future? What is the probability that you will get at most one correct answer?" The connection between relative frequency and probability is typically not automatic for many students, so you will need to make this point explicit.

Extend: Discuss as a class the nature of obtaining empirical results, and have students brainstorm ideas on simulations like this one that might be useful. Then lead a discussion in which students suggest at least three other real-world examples that are mathematically equivalent to this problem.

Teacher Support for Extend: Once you are assured that students understand how to create and conduct the simulation, help students aggregate the data from the entire class. Then discuss the theoretical probabilities and have students compare their results with those produced by the binomial distribution. If desired, introduce the Law of Large Numbers; be sure that students clearly understand that the more trials, the better.

Students should also be expected to describe other contexts for which this simulation would work. For example, students might think of the probability of having a certain number of boys or girls in a family with four children, passing through four unsynchronized green traffic lights, having rain on four different days when the weather forecast calls for a 50 percent chance of rain, or winning a certain number of games against an evenly matched opponent.

The latter three examples might lead to a new simulation in which the probability of any one success is no longer 50 percent. A random number generator on a calculator can be helpful. For example, suppose you are playing cards and the probability of winning any one game is 32 percent; suppose further that you plan to play five games. The calculator could generate five random integers from 1 to 100, inclusive, and you could designate that any value from 1 to 32 represents a win and any value from 33 to 100 represents a loss. You could then count the number of wins for five games to represent a single trial of the experiment.

Adaptations: You can restrict the simulation to flipping coins if using multiple strategies will distract students from focusing on the probabilities. For more advanced students or those who finish early, present the same challenge, but instead of true/false questions, the students are guessing blindly on multiple-choice questions with five choices. Students' intuitions about probability likely range widely, so be prepared to help students with fundamental ideas, including randomization and assigning numerical values to probabilities. For example, you may select two students and have them flip a coin, with one student flipping and the other calling heads or tails. Lead students into collecting data on the successes one of the students has and developing strategies for displaying the data. As students work on the simulation for this lesson, confirm that every student understands that on each question, our concern is not whether the answer is true or false, but whether the student got it right or wrong (this may require a discussion with the entire class).

Mathematics Lesson 2: Where Should We Meet?

This problem was presented as a sample math lesson in Chapter 4 (p. 62), and its details are not repeated here. Through investigation, students discover that the median is not only the 50th percentile but also the value that minimizes the total distance to all of the data points in a set. Instead of simply being told that it is often better to use the median when a data set is skewed (such "rules" are often overused and misused; sharing them should depend on the purpose as to which measure of center to use), students discover this attribute as they develop their skills in organizing and displaying data. Also, they continue to develop their number sense as they learn through experience that a measure of center is a value that summarizes a data set in a way that can solve real-world problems.

Mathematics Lesson 3: What Score Do You Need?

Key Concepts: The mean as "center of gravity"; deviations

Common Core State Standards: Recognize that a measure of center summarizes all of the values in a data set; relate choice of measure of center to the context and what the measure indicates.

Objective: Students will discover that the positive and negative deviations from the mean in any data set sum to 0. Applying this idea, they will determine a value that is needed to achieve a desired mean.

Essential Question: What score do you need on the final exam to obtain the desired mean?

Lesson Overview: Students will calculate a mean for different sets of numbers, find the positive and negative deviations from the mean for each value, and then determine what score is needed to achieve a given target mean (final score).

Engage: Ask students how they might determine their test average for a grading period. You should discover if they recognize that different measures of center can be used and if they know how to determine any of these centers. You can also ask students to find the mean of two fairly large values that are reasonably close together, such as the mean of $20,642 and $20,658. Do students use only the commonly taught algorithm that would have them sum the values and divide by 2; or do they realize that with a difference of $16, the mean must be $8 more than $20,642 and $8 less than $20,658? To ensure that students can address the idea of positive and negative deviations on an intuitive level, pose questions like these: "If a book weighs 8 pounds, how far off, and in what direction, were two students who estimated the weight at 5 pounds and 15 pounds?" If students can't provide a satisfactory answer, then offer some explicit instruction before they begin the Explore phase.

Teacher Support for Engage: One purpose of the Engage is to determine if students have some intuitive feel for the mean as the center of balance. We assume that students have had some prior exposure to finding the mean of a set of numbers, having received instruction in the process of summing the values and dividing by the number of values. Probe for the depth of their understanding. If, for example, they sum 118 and 124 and divide by 2 to find their mean, you should include a preliminary Explore-Explain sequence with pairs of numbers, asking explicit questions of the students such as "Now that you've found the mean is 121, how do 118 and 124 compare to this mean?" Several examples may be necessary until students discover that they can look for a value that is the same distance above one of the values as it is below the other. From working with pairs of numbers, include an additional Explore-Explain sequence addressing similar questions when there are three values in the data set.

Explore 1 (summing the deviations): Working in pairs, students receive a set of test scores (e.g., 78, 96, 93, 82, 98, 80, and 89) and compute the mean. Then ask them to identify how many scores are below the mean and how many are above the mean. Next have them consider all the scores below the mean and determine how far below each score is. They then find the sum of these deviations. Similarly, they find the deviations of all of the scores above the mean and sum these deviations. They should reflect on what they have found and form a conjecture. To test their conjecture, have students create their own set of scores and verify whether the conjecture holds true. Allow the students to use calculators for this exploration, because the focus should be on the concepts concerning the deviations, not the calculations.

Teacher Support for Explore 1: During this Explore, students are addressing a common misconception: that the number of values below the mean must equal the number of values above the mean. Students should be encouraged to create their own sets of values that meet certain criteria. For example, ask them to find a set of six numbers for which two are below the mean and four are above the mean, or a set of five numbers for which four are below the mean and one is above the mean. With additional exercises and enough opportunities to explore the underlying concepts, students are more likely to overcome any misconceptions.

Explain 1: Students should explain, with your facilitation, their conjectures and what they found when they tested these conjectures.

Teacher Support for Explain 1: Most of the explanations should come from the students as they report their results; you should challenge not only the students who are presenting but the others in class about generalizing the ideas: "Can there be the same number of values above and below the mean? Why?" "Can all of the values be below the mean? Why?" "Can you find an example where the sum of the deviations below the mean does not equal the sum of deviations above the mean? Why?" Before proceeding, students should have developed two ideas: (1) the number of scores below the mean and the number of scores above the mean do not have to be equal, and (2) the sum of the deviations below the mean (the negative deviations) are always balanced by the sum of the deviations above the mean (the positive deviations); in other words, the sum of all the deviations from the mean is always 0.

Explore 2 (finding a missing score): Working in pairs, students determine what score they would need on the final exam in order for their average to be 90, given that the other test scores were 78, 96, 93, 82, 98, 80, and 89.

Teacher Support for Explore 2: For this Explore, the teacher should ensure that students explore two strategies: (1) determine the total number of points needed over eight tests to produce an average of 90, and then determine what score is needed on the final test to obtain this number; and (2) sum all the deviations from the desired mean of 90 and determine the value needed so that the total deviation will be 0. However, you should not explain these specific strategies, but instead prompt students with questions. For example, when they try to find the second strategy, prompt with questions such as "What is the sum of deviations from the target mean before the final test? What does the sum of deviations ultimately have to be? What score might achieve this?"

Students should summarize these two strategies, explaining why they work the way they do. Many students will have received prior instruction in the first strategy, which requires more of an algebraic approach (because the sum of the values divided by the number of values equals the mean, the sum of the values must equal the product of the number of values and the mean), but they may not have made sense of it. Through leading questions, ensure that students make the connection to the formula they have been told previously. The second strategy can be used to develop students' intuitive understanding of positive and negative numbers as well as their understanding of the mean, so prepare to ask guiding questions as students tackle this Explore activity. You may decide to split this second Explore into two separate parts, each of which would be followed by its own Explain.

Explain 2: With teacher prompts leading to significant classroom discourse, students should explain both solution strategies. Afterward, pose a couple of questions so that students can consider which strategy is easier mentally, and which is easier if the values are reasonably close to each other.

Extend: After the students have had several opportunities to practice and apply their new concepts and you are confident that every student understands, ask the following question: "What if there are two tests left instead of one? Specifically, what would you need on the final two tests to obtain a mean score of 90 if your first seven scores were 78, 96, 93, 82, 98, 80, and 89?" After reflecting on this question, students should come to realize how powerful the second strategy is. Because their first seven scores resulted in a total deviation of −14 from a mean of 90, as long as their next two tests produce a deviation of +14 from 90, they will have achieved their desired mean. For example, if they score 96 on the next test, which is 6 points above 90, they will need a 98 on the next test so that they will have recaptured all 14 points they need. They should also realize that if they score, say, 91, on the eighth test, unless there is extra credit and it is possible to score more than 100, their dream has been shattered, as it would take 103 points to bring the mean up to 90.

Teacher Support for Extend: This Extend section is directed at reinforcing the idea of the deviations from the mean. Ask students to find the final test scores to achieve a mean when two or even three tests are missing. It may also be helpful to use students' current grades. For example, suppose they have taken three tests in the grading period, with two more left before the marking period is over. You might ask them what scores they would need on the final two tests so that their test average would be 90, 80, 70, or 60. Students could also create their own problems of this nature.

Also, as you reinforce the ideas during this Extend, present students with different contexts, such as the number of hours of sleep they might need to average 9 hours per night, or the number of hours they have to study so that they have averaged 1.5 hours per day.

Adaptations: For students not yet ready for the context provided earlier, start with some type of "math balance" scale. With this type of balance, available from many educational suppliers, students can add different weights at various distances from zero in either direction. Ideally, this initial exploration should be conducted in elementary grades, but it can serve as an excellent manipulative tool to help students explore and develop the idea that the total deviations from the middle in both directions must balance themselves out. From there, you may want to bring up the idea of a teeter-totter, for which the lighter child must sit farther from the center than the heavier child. After these initial explorations, students should be ready to explore the mean when it is not centered at zero. A challenge for more advanced students is to have them create a spreadsheet that shows the current mean, the total deviations from a target mean, and an additional value that will result in the target mean.

Pay particular attention—and come back occasionally—to the idea that there do not need to be the same numbers of values below the mean as there are above the mean, but that the total deviations below the mean must be equivalent to the total deviations above the mean. Extreme examples, such as a company with four workers who make $10,000, $10,000, $10,000, and $90,000, might help solidify this idea. For younger students or those for whom mathematics has not been about sense making, multiple opportunities with a math balance and small sets of low-value numbers may be needed to drive home the idea of positive and negative deviations.

Mathematics Lesson 4: Curving Your Grades

Key Concepts: Measures of center and measures of spread; effects of transformations on these measures

Common Core State Standards: Summarize numerical data sets in their context. Connect geometric, algebraic, and statistical transformations.

Objective: Students will determine what happens to common measures of center and spread when data sets are transformed through translations and dilations.

Essential Question: What happens to measures of center when 10 points are added to each value in a set of test scores?

Lesson Overview: Working either individually or in pairs, students explore what happens to measures of center and measures of dispersion (spread) when a teacher "curves" a test by (1) adding 10 points to everyone's grade and (2) adding 10 percent of the original score to everyone's grade.

Engage: Begin with a short pretest to determine whether students understand the two types of transformations under consideration (translation: adding 10 points to each grade; and dilation: adding 10 percent of the original score to each grade) and whether they can predict what happens to the measures of center and measures of spread. The results will influence the direction you take.

Teacher Support for Engage: During Engage, probe for prior knowledge and misconceptions. If students do not recognize that measures of center are a way of summarizing an entire data set with a representative value or values or if they do not know how to find measures of center, then students are not ready to explore. Also determine whether students recognize that measures of center are not fully sufficient to assess a data set. For example, knowing that the yearly mean temperature for an entire region is 70 degrees would be insufficient if a person wants to know the temperatures for a specific city. One may also like to know the temperature variation for that city.

Explore: Working alone or in groups of two, students explore the Curving Your Grades exercise that follows and then prepare a written presentation of their findings. Depending on students' proficiency with technology, the Explore activity can take anywhere from 30 minutes to 90 minutes; calculators may allow students to focus on the questions and not the calculations.

Curving Your Grades

Suppose that the 20 students take a quiz on statistics. The scores are shown in the following frequency table.

Score	40	72	78	80	82	84	86	88	90
Frequency	1	2	3	4	2	1	1	4	2

1. Without performing any calculations, use the table to determine the mode, the range of scores, the median, and the interquartile range (IQR). Then verify with a calculator.

2. Estimate the mean. Then verify with a calculator.

Because of an error on the quiz, your teacher decides to "curve" the scores and is considering two plans. For option 1, your teacher will add 10 points to each student's score. For option 2, your teacher will add 10% of the original number of points to each student's score.

3. For option 1, determine what happens to the mean, the median, the mode, the range of scores, and the IQR.

4. For option 2, determine what happens to the mean, the median, the mode, the range of scores, and the IQR.

5. Construct a boxplot for the three sets of scores on the same set of axes. Comment on the changes that the options cause to the graphs. What kind of transformations are these?

6. When do you believe option 1 is fairer? When do you believe option 2 is fairer? Explain.

Teacher Support for Explore: If students have the prerequisite knowledge and skills, then they should be able to explore without much guidance. To keep students on track, challenge them to defend their findings and ask questions such as "Why do you think this is what happens?"

For early finishers, have students determine whether other graphical representations would represent the results well; particularly with histograms, for which the width of the intervals can be altered, this can be a meaningful and challenging exploration.

Explain: After students submit their work, lead a discussion in which students develop a solid understanding that option 1 is a translation (a "slide") of the data, so the measures of center all increase by 10 points, but the distance between the values remains unchanged. For option 2, you should ask questions so that students understand that someone who initially scored 0 will have 0 points added, while someone who scored 100 will have 10 points added. This should help students see why both the measures of center and the measures of spread increase by 10 percent. The boxplots constructed in part 5 of the lesson should help solidify these ideas, while discussion in part 6 should help students understand the two different options and the circumstances that might influence the decision as to which one is fairer.

Teacher Support for Explain: During the Explain, challenge the students' results by asking why things happen as they do. Ask very explicit questions, such as "What transformation that you have studied is equivalent to adding 10 points to each person's grade? What transformation is equivalent to adding 10 percent of the original score to each person's grade?" Showing geometric translations and dilations may help students visualize the transformations that are occurring. Emphasize the preservation of distance for the translation and the change of distance for the dilation. Placing individual points on a number line may also help students make sense of the transformations, perhaps with the addition of 0 and 100 to the original set of scores.

The discussion as to which option is fairer should also solidify students' understanding. Though I advocate accepting a variety of opinions here, the discussion may include statements such as the following: "Suppose there was a 10-point question that everyone missed and was not covered in the material; in this circumstance, everyone should receive an extra 10 points. Alternatively, suppose the test was fair but challenging. Those who worked harder did better and thus deserve a greater reward."

Extend: To ensure that students are not only answering the questions but understanding the underlying concepts, pose the following questions.

1. In general, what happens to the mean, median, mode, range, and IQR of any group of scores if x units are added to each value in a data set?

2. In general, what happens to the mean, median, mode, range, and IQR of any group of scores if y percent of the original value is added to each value in a data set?

Teacher Support for Extend: The Extend section is intended to ensure that students have internalized and generalized the ideas. If the algebraic form of the question interferes with students' ability to address the issue, ask about the measures of center and measures of spread using different contexts. For example, you might ask about these measures if a company gives each employee a $3,000 raise or if the company gives each employee a 5 percent raise. Students may also come up with their own scenarios. This discussion could lead to considering whether raises (or taxes, library fees, or other monetary amounts) should be based on set amounts or on relative amounts.

After several examples, push toward using symbols to represent the mathematical ideas:

1. If x units are added to each value in a data set, then the mean, median, and mode are all increased by x units; however, the range and IQR remain unchanged, though their lowest and highest values are increased by x points.

2. If y percent of the original value is added to each value in a data set, then the mean, median, mode, range, and IQR are all increased by y percent.

Adaptations: If graphing calculators are not available, then you may want to use scores up to 10, rather than up to 100. For less experienced students, some more fundamental instruction or investigation may be needed, particularly in regard to measures of spread, prior to Explore. For more advanced students, the dilation (option 2) can be based on a value other than 0 (e.g., adding 10 percent to each student's grade for each point away from 50, thus lowering the scores below 50 and increasing the scores above 50). Another adaption is in the measures that are used; you may want to include the mean absolute deviation and standard deviation in the explorations.

The prior knowledge and possible misconceptions that students bring into this investigation will significantly affect your decisions;

consequently, Engage is even more important than usual. Students who do not yet understand the measures of center and fundamental measures of spread (specifically range and interquartile range) are not yet ready and should receive instruction on these topics first.

This chapter has explored two unique units of study, one in science and one in mathematics. The approaches taken for each unit demonstrate the dynamic nature of inquiry-based instruction. Although very different in the overall construction of the units, the core of having students Explore core ideas before Explanation was retained. The science unit used more of a developmental approach where ideas continued to build on one another as the inquiry-based project progressed. For the mathematics unit, each of the lessons within the unit helped to reinforce the learning involved in the core idea, but each lesson was discrete and could be taught without others. Each mathematics lesson in the unit provided a new or additional aspect associated with chance or probability events. Now that we have considered the curriculum and planning, our attention will shift in the next chapter to the implementation of the lesson.

3

Succeeding with
INQUIRY
Instruction

6

How Successful Was Your Inquiry Lesson Today?

There is no magic elixir that will instantly eliminate all the challenges that prevent immediate success with all students. However, wouldn't it be nice to know if what you did in the classroom today will positively affect student achievement as the year progresses?

Well, help is available. My colleagues and I have identified 19 performance indicators that teachers can control that influence student achievement (Marshall, Smart, & Horton, 2010). These indicators are divided into four factors of teaching effectiveness that successful teachers must master to maximize learning:

- Instruction (How do you facilitate learning?)
- Discourse (How are the environment and interactions structured?)
- Assessment (How do you know when students are successful?)
- Curriculum (How do students interact with the concepts?)

To help teachers assess their own practice through the 19 indicators, we developed the Electronic Quality of Inquiry Protocol (EQUIP).* Developed

---

*You can access EQUIP using these options: (1) Download the free pdf file from www.clemson.edu/iim. Select the research and evaluation tab, then select EQUIP. (2) Download the free app from the Apple Store. Search for "EQUIP (Inquiry Protocol)", which will then let you store observations directly on your tablet or (3) Download the app and link all project data to a personalized database (see www.clemson.edu/iim for instructions).

and refined over five years (Marshall et al., 2010), this free tool provides teachers with a snapshot of how successful a given lesson is in terms of inquiry-based instruction. To underscore what is being measured, here again is the definition of inquiry-based instruction we are using:

> **Inquiry-based instruction** is the development of understanding through investigation—that is, asking questions, determining appropriate methods, gathering data, thinking critically about relationships between evidence and explanations, and formulating and communicating logical arguments. (adapted from the National Science Education Standards, NRC, 1996, p. 105)

Although the protocol seeks to measure the degree of success only for inquiry-based teaching and learning, it has been shown to be a solid predictor of overall student achievement, in terms of both content and process knowledge (Marshall, 2012; Marshall, Horton, & Padilla, 2012). Thus, inquiry-based forms of learning, when done well, can increase student achievement in terms of both factual, rote memory (typical achievement tests) and analytical, critical thinking forms of learning—the best of both worlds (Blanchard et al., 2010; Furtak, Seidel, Iverson, & Briggs, 2012; Minner, Levy, & Century, 2009; Wilson et al., 2009).

Undoubtedly, we must help students learn facts, algorithms, and definitions, but meaningful learning also entails all students going beyond rote learning to think critically about the material, make connections to prior learning, and apply ideas and insights to new situations. The teacher is the essential factor in achieving rigorous, meaningful learning, and evidence suggests that an inquiry-based approach can stimulate and develop critical thinking while helping students master key facts and algorithms (Donovan & Bransford, 2005; Llewellyn, 2002; Marshall & Horton, 2011; NRC, 2000).

As we've seen, the 4E × 2 Instructional Model (Marshall, Horton, & Edmondson, 2007; Marshall et al., 2009) and the lessons described in previous chapters can help teachers design and implement a rich instructional sequence. However, simply saying that one uses an inquiry-based approach is not enough to ensure that effective high-quality inquiry is actually occurring. Teachers also need good assessments to help them scaffold their own performance, making improvements and filtering out low-value instructional activities. To that end, EQUIP provides the next layer needed to help transform instructional practice.

EQUIP Overview

Good teachers use many different instructional methods throughout a day, week, and year. EQUIP is not designed for all situations; it targets the factors associated with the quality of inquiry-based instruction, not other methods that may be used in the classroom. My advice is to use EQUIP to obtain a solid point of reference that honestly reflects what you are doing in the classroom. Once you have established this benchmark, use the protocol to help develop a plan to raise the level of your own performance.

EQUIP addresses aspects that relate to the four specific factors that support inquiry-based teaching and learning: Instruction, Discourse, Assessment, and Curriculum. Each indicator has four possible performance levels:

- Pre-inquiry (level 1)
- Developing Inquiry (level 2)
- Proficient Inquiry (level 3)
- Exemplary Inquiry (level 4)

A descriptive rubric provides explicit detail for every indicator at each level. These descriptions not only guide the assessment scoring but also provide a target for individual teachers, departments, or schools. Level 3 or above should be the target if highly effective inquiry is the goal, but there are times when level 1 or 2 lessons may be needed. For instance, if you are working with a group of students who have little prior inquiry learning experience, then jumping into a level 3 or 4 lesson would likely result in students shutting down—you have placed them into cognitive overload. In such cases, inquiry learning needs to be scaffolded until students' comfort level increases. Additionally, when assessing your lessons, try not to become defensive about the ratings but, rather, seek to understand why a score falls into a specific level and what you can do to advance to a higher level.

After a lesson, the teacher or observer scoring the rubric determines the level of inquiry demonstrated on each of the 19 total indicators. The complete list of the 19 indicators and an abbreviated rubric can be found in the appendix.

Once you have a benchmark measurement, then you can begin to chart your growth and target the areas for improvement, working alone or with a team of teachers (see Chapter 8). This process helps move from the vague "I know it when I see it" opinion to a deep understanding of the specific aspects of a lesson that make inquiry effective.

You can use EQUIP in several ways to assess teaching performance:

• *Basic reflection:* Simply reflecting on a lesson is the most convenient option but also the most subjective and least likely to bring about transformation in your practice.

• *Video analysis:* You can video-record a lesson and assess it by watching the video and using the EQUIP rubric. Although we are often hypercritical when watching videos of ourselves, this professional development exercise will reveal many things about your teaching practice—if you let it. To emphasize the value of this exercise, National Board Certification and the Presidential Award for Excellence in Mathematics and Science Teaching require a self-analysis of a video-recorded lesson as a significant part of the application process.

• *Peer evaluation:* You can have another teacher or instructional coach complete EQUIP after observing one of your classes. Promoting healthy dialogue, this option gives you insights that you might miss without another set of eyes. However, ground rules need to be established so that teachers don't overstep the boundaries. For instance, the observation and subsequent discussion should focus on observations and justifications for only the 19 indicators and not other elements of a colleague's teaching or classroom. Better still, after scoring all 19 indicators, select 2–3 to focus on for a deeper discussion.

• *Departmental study:* An instructional coach or curriculum coordinator can use EQUIP to guide conversations with a teacher or team of teachers. This approach is especially beneficial in helping departments or schools target critical topics as part of professional development. If a department or group of teachers wants to use EQUIP, then a group training session is essential to establish interrater agreement. Otherwise, one person's score is not generalizable to the others in the group.

As a classroom teacher, you can gain important information about your own practice related to inquiry-based instruction using EQUIP. Additionally, visit the Inquiry in Motion website to watch several videos, with lesson analysis keys: www.clemson.edu/iim/lessonplans. After a quick and free registration, you can log in and access information under the EQUIP training tab.

Examples of Assessments

Let's look at some sample assessments of the two unit lessons described in Chapter 5 to help you understand the four factors—Instruction, Discourse, Assessment, and Curriculum. To quickly summarize, the physical science lesson on motion, Mousetrap Racers, is framed by the essential question "What factors affect the motion of an object?" Small student groups must create a mousetrap racer that would go five meters at most but would stop before six meters. This activity incorporates process skills (e.g., asking good scientific questions, collecting meaningful data, analyzing results) and conceptual ideas (e.g., speed, motion, force, conservation of energy) from science, math, technology, and engineering (Marshall et al., 2009).

The mathematics example, "Where Should We Meet?" asks where five police officers should meet to minimize the total distance traveled if they individually begin at mile markers 2, 4, 16, 28, and 50. After this problem is solved, a sixth officer is added at mile marker 80; the question remains the same. Students are expected to generalize and in some way demonstrate a proof of their results. They determine important characteristics of measures of center while refining their process skills, including problem solving, determining an appropriate method, organizing information, communicating, and mathematical reasoning.

Factor 1: Instruction

Figure 6.1 shows two of the five indicators that compose the factor of Instruction. Because the indicators are associated with the same factor, there are connections among them. However, these connections are not absolute; there are sufficient distinctions among the indicators so that the levels often vary considerably even within the same factor.

Sample Lesson in Science

The teacher gave vehicle assembly instructions before students had sufficient time to think through their own creation and stopped and lectured about the terminology associated with motion. So the Instructional Strategies indicator earned a level 2 inquiry rating. Had the teacher provided more opportunities for students to share their ideas throughout the investigation, then the quality of the inquiry would have been at least level 3.

The teacher did achieve a level 3 inquiry rating for Order of Instruction: the lesson engaged the students in exploring concepts before the teacher explained them, and students were involved in explaining their conceptual ideas to the teacher and their peers.

Figure 6.1
Examples of Indicators Associated with Inquiry Instruction

Indicator Measured	Instructional Factors			
	Pre-inquiry (Level 1)	Developing Inquiry (Level 2)	Proficient Inquiry (Level 3)	Exemplary Inquiry (Level 4)
Instructional Strategies	Teacher predominantly lectured to cover content.	Teacher frequently lectured or used demonstrations to explain content. Activities were verification only.	Teacher occasionally lectured, but students were engaged in activities that helped develop conceptual understanding.	Teacher occasionally lectured, but students were engaged in investigations that promoted strong conceptual understanding.
Order of Instruction	Teacher explained concepts. Students either did not explore concepts or did so only after explanation.	Teacher asked students to explore concepts before receiving explanation. Teacher explained.	Teacher asked students to explore before explanation. Teacher and students explained.	Teacher asked students to explore concepts before explanation occurred. Although perhaps prompted by the teacher, students provided the explanation.

Sample Lesson in Math

This class was rated level 3 on Instructional Strategies. Although the Engage part of the lesson was minimal, the teacher presented the problem and gave the students, who were working in groups of three, a considerable amount of time to develop the ideas for themselves in the Explore phase. She gave them several prompts to challenge their thinking and to push them toward the underlying ideas. The lesson did not reach level 4 because the teacher used lecture rather than the investigation to promote conceptual understanding. However, the lesson was above level 2 because the students were discovering the ideas for themselves.

For Order of Instruction, the lesson earned a level 2 rating. After a solid Explore phase during which students were developing the conceptual ideas, the teacher lectured the class with only minimal participation by students. She told them what they should have found and what the underlying principles were, and then provided an informal proof of these principles. To earn a higher rating, the students would have played a much greater role in this explanation, with the teacher guiding them only as necessary.

Evaluating Your Own Class

Changing the order of instruction so that Explore precedes Explain is likely the largest transformation that you will make relative to inquiry-based instruction. Consider how you taught a key concept this past week. Did you allow students to interact with the problem, concept, or ideas first, or did you feel compelled to explain it to students first? Regardless, look ahead to tomorrow or next week.

TIP Explore-before-Explain

Think of an upcoming lesson where you could allow students to explore, with some guidance, a concept before you provided an explanation. What is the concept being studied, what is the objective for the lesson, and how will the Explore tie to the concept?

Remember that abrupt changes to how students have been learning (or how you teach) are likely to bump up against some resistance unless you scaffold the new approach. In addition, lecture can indeed be appropriate; it is the amount of lecture and where it occurs in the lesson, not its presence or absence, that are important.

Factor 2: Discourse

Discourse measures the classroom climate and interactions relating to inquiry instruction and learning. Two of the five indicators associated with this factor are shown in Figure 6.2.

Figure 6.2
Discourse Indicators Associated with Inquiry Instruction

Indicator Measured	Discourse Factors			
	Pre-inquiry (Level 1)	Developing Inquiry (Level 2)	Proficient Inquiry (Level 3)	Exemplary Inquiry (Level 4)
Questioning Level	Questioning rarely challenged students above the remembering level.	Questioning rarely challenged students above the understanding level.	Questioning challenged students up to application or analysis levels.	Questioning challenged students at various levels, including at the analysis level or higher; level was varied to scaffold learning.
Classroom Interaction	Teacher accepted answers, correcting when necessary, but rarely followed up with further probing.	Teacher or another student occasionally followed up student response with further low-level probe.	Teacher or another student often followed up response with engaging probe that required student to justify reasoning or evidence.	Teacher consistently and effectively facilitated rich classroom dialogue where evidence, assumptions, and reasoning were challenged by teacher or other students.

Sample Lesson in Science

As the lesson progressed, the teacher asked challenging, higher-level questions (e.g., "How did your results compare with those from other groups?") as students presented their findings, which resulted in a level 3 rating for Questioning Level. However, once students responded to the higher-level questions, the quality of the interactions dropped as the teacher followed up responses with only low-level probes (e.g., "How did you find the second point on the graph?"). This resulted in a rating of level 2 for Classroom Interaction. The teacher could improve by following up student responses with more thought-provoking questions, such as "Why was the slope calculated by group 2 larger than the slope calculated by group 1? What does that slope tell us?"

Sample Lesson in Math

Although the prompts given for the problem were challenging and had the potential to develop deep understanding, the Questioning Level received only a level 2 rating. The teacher asked questions such as "What would happen if the original five mile markers were different?" but did not go beyond expecting the students to state simply that the officers should meet at the middle mile marker. The teacher explained the concepts at deeper levels but did not involve the students in significant discourse. The lesson was above level 1, however, because the teacher did expect students to think more deeply than simply recalling what they had found.

Classroom Interaction was rated at level 1. The teacher asked questions that had short, direct answers and did not follow them up with probing questions or by asking other students to respond.

Evaluating Your Own Class

Many nuances are associated with solid discourse in the classroom, but just a few clear changes can have dramatic positive effects on learning. For instance, thinking back to your last lesson, what were three typical questions that you asked? What could you have asked that would have challenged students to think at a higher level? Think about creating three "pocket" questions (i.e., you pull them out of your pocket, virtual or actual, as needed) that you can use in every class period to challenge your students to think beyond rote memorization.

Also consider whether the discourse in your last lesson more answer focused (e.g., "What is the answer to exercise 3?"; "What is the function of the nucleus?") or evidence focused (e.g., "How did you determine the speed of the vehicle?"; "Describe how you graphed the equation"). Generally speaking, to improve classroom discourse, aim for more "how" and "why" questions and fewer "what" questions.

Factor 3: Assessment

Five indicators are used to measure the Assessment factor relating to instructional practice. Two of the indicators are shown in Figure 6.3.

Figure 6.3
Assessment Indicators Associated with Inquiry Instruction

Indicator Measured	Assessment Factors			
	Pre-inquiry (Level 1)	Developing Inquiry (Level 2)	Proficient Inquiry (Level 3)	Exemplary Inquiry (Level 4)
Prior Knowledge	Teacher did not assess students' prior knowledge.	Teacher assessed students' prior knowledge but did not modify instruction based on this knowledge.	Teacher assessed students' prior knowledge and then partially modified instruction based on this knowledge.	Teacher assessed students' prior knowledge and then modified instruction based on this knowledge.
Conceptual Development	Teacher encouraged learning by memorization and repetition.	Teacher encouraged product- or answer-focused learning activities that lacked critical thinking.	Teacher encouraged process-focused learning activities that required critical thinking.	Teacher encouraged process-focused learning activities that involved critical thinking that connected learning with other concepts.

Sample Lesson in Science

The teacher did not attempt to assess or take into consideration her students' prior knowledge, so the lesson earned a level 1 inquiry rating for Prior Knowledge. A short pretest, a KWL chart, or even a discussion on what students already knew may have revealed strengths and misconceptions about motion.

The teacher received a level 2 rating on Conceptual Development. When formative assessments are integral to the teaching and learning process, student learning increases (Black, Harrison, Lee, Marshall, & Wiliam, 2004). By making the lesson more prescribed than necessary, the teacher minimized critical thinking. If students had been challenged to defend their solutions to scientific questions, a level 3 or 4 rating would be appropriate.

Sample Lesson in Math

The math lesson received the same low ratings as the science lesson. Prior Knowledge was rated at level 1 because the teacher did not ask students what they knew about the characteristics of center or ask them to make predictions about the answer.

Conceptual Development earned a level 2 rating, but this was a difficult determination because the observer could not easily tell whether the teacher wanted students to simply memorize that the median is the measure of center that minimizes the total distance to the data points (which would have earned a level 1 score), or whether he expected the students to understand the result because of how the ideas had been developed. Because of the strong Explore phase preceding the explanation of the underlying concepts, he earned a level 2 for this aspect of the lesson. Had the Explain phase involved the students more in using their exploration to determine the underlying concepts, the lesson could have earned a level 3 rating.

Evaluating Your Own Class

Effectively and frequently using formative assessments is one of the most critical changes that teachers can make that will lead to increased student achievement. However, to be clear, it is only formative assessment when you intentionally *act* on the data you have collected.

This may mean proceeding as you planned, but the quality of the assessment and the intentionality of your actions are what make formative assessments so valuable in targeting your teaching.

TIP Formative Assessment Tomorrow

Thinking ahead to tomorrow's lesson, what are three ways that you can formatively check for student understanding from every student? Asking a question during a class discussion does not count because you only hear from one student at a time, and usually only the students who know the answers will respond. What about all the other students—do they get it, too? Finally, how will you modify your instruction if students clearly are still confused by the concept or algorithm?

Factor 4: Curriculum

Four indicators are associated with the Curriculum factor related to inquiry instruction. These indicators are tied directly to what is experienced by students, not what appears in a text or notes. Organizing and Recording Information is one of several areas in which teachers can deliver different levels of scaffolding, thus differentiating instruction. The goal is to challenge all students to their highest level without frustrating anyone. For instance, one student with a learning disability may need the structure that a graphic organizer provides, whereas an ESL student may need more visuals to help decode the language barriers. We should always strive to help students progress to a level where less direct assistance is needed. By doing so, we will have encouraged habits of lifelong learning. To earn level 4 on this and other indicators, consider the various needs of *all* students in your class. Two of the Curriculum indicators, Integration of Content and Investigation and Organizing and Recording Information, are displayed in Figure 6.4.

Sample Lesson in Science

The Integration of Content and Investigation earned a level 3 inquiry rating because the lesson almost continually integrated concepts such as speed versus time graphs and conservation of energy into the student investigations. Organizing and Recording Information was scored at level 2 because the teacher gave students little opportunity to determine how the data should be collected and organized. When data sheets are provided with the headings and axes already labeled (which was the case during this observation), students are deprived of a rich opportunity to think about how to collect, organize, and convey meaning from the data. By organizing and recording information as they see fit, students can think more deeply and more critically about the concepts being investigated (e.g., "How many trials are needed? Is speed the independent or dependent variable, and why?"). Had the teacher provided this opportunity, the rating for this indicator would have risen to a level 3 or 4.

Figure 6.4
Curriculum Indicators Associated with Inquiry Instruction

Indicator Measured	Curriculum Factors			
	Pre-inquiry (Level 1)	Developing Inquiry (Level 2)	Proficient Inquiry (Level 3)	Exemplary Inquiry (Level 4)
Integration of Content and Investigation	Lesson either content focused or activity focused but not both.	Lesson provided poor integration of content with activity or investigation.	Lesson incorporated student investigation that linked well with content.	Lesson seamlessly integrated the content and the student investigation.
Organizing and Recording Information	Students organized and recorded information in prescriptive ways.	Students had only minor input as to how to organize and record information.	Students regularly organized and recorded information in nonprescriptive ways.	Students organized and recorded information in nonprescriptive ways that allowed them to effectively communicate their learning.

Sample Lesson in Math

The lesson had an excellent activity and was targeted at important mathematical content, but these two facets of the class were not well integrated. After the investigation, the teacher explained the concepts without much student input and did not clearly guide the students in mastering the underlying ideas based on their findings. Consequently, the lesson earned a level 2 rating on Integration of Content and Investigation.

The class earned a level 3 rating on Organizing and Recording Information. During the Explore phase, the teacher encouraged the students to organize their data in some logical manner and to make sure they had records of all of their attempts, but she did not tell them how to do this. The lesson fell short of a level 4 because the students did not use their data to communicate to the teacher or other students, in either oral or written form, what they had learned.

Evaluating Your Own Class

As your students left class today, could they explicitly and accurately tell how today's lesson fits into the bigger picture of learning in your class? Or would they just tell you, "Today we learned about triangles [or amphibians—fill in the topic]," with no clear connection to other concepts studied, the real world, or anything of relevance to the student?

TIP Building Self-Reliance

What are two explicit ways that you can help students better recognize how their daily learning fits into the bigger picture of mastery in your class? How can you help students begin moving from dependence on you for everything (e.g., data tables, notes, definitions) to greater self-reliance in organizing and collecting information? This latter goal is critical for lifelong learning.

Improving the Quality of Inquiry Teaching

After each of the indicators associated with the four factors in EQUIP are assessed, a holistic rating is determined for each factor. This holistic rating is not necessarily the mean of the indicators but is the level that best captures the essence of the lesson. Although approaching the rating this way may seem overly subjective, I have found that interrater reliability (consistency between different raters) is typically quite high.

Completing the instrument for a specific lesson provides an assessment of the current state of inquiry instruction in your classroom. The next step is to improve the quality of inquiry. Establishing a benchmark may bring about some change just by having specific aspects of instructional practice brought to your attention, but our goal is to become more intentional and explicit by developing an action plan of next steps.

I recommend that you focus on one specific indicator (not even an entire factor) that you want to improve during the next lesson or unit of study. Once you have achieved that growth, then address another indicator. After four indicators relating to inquiry instruction have been improved—perhaps one from each of the Instruction, Discourse, Assessment, and Curriculum factors—try to maintain that level of performance before tackling more improvements. If teachers at your school work together and note common areas for growth, then it may make sense to also work on certain indicators together. This shared approach provides a support structure to exchange thoughts and ideas. (See Chapter 8 for tips on creating an improvement plan.)

If your current teaching practice falls largely in level 1, you may want to begin by reading about constructivist approaches to learning and inquiry-based methods of teaching, looking for examples of lessons and instruction. Many articles from the National Science Teachers Association and the National Council of Teachers of Mathematics and journals (e.g., *The Science Teacher*, *The Mathematics Teacher*), along with publications from other professional organizations, provide several other innovative ideas. (See the reference list at the end of this book for starters.) Also, seek out any of the professional development institutes that offer opportunities to experience inquiry learning firsthand.

Generally, a level 2 performance suggests that a teacher is familiar with getting students engaged and active, but the lessons tend to be more prescriptive, with students having only limited opportunities to develop ideas or make sense of results for themselves. Instruction is still heavily teacher focused.

At level 3, the teacher has demonstrated a student-centered, inquiry-based learning environment that actively engages students in investigations, questions, and explanations. The teacher's role remains vital (as it does at all levels), but the teacher now functions more as a facilitator who scaffolds learning experiences than as a giver of facts and knowledge.

I do not expect that any one lesson would merit a level 4 for all indicators or even for all factors. In fact, I have yet to see such a lesson—and

I have seen some amazing lessons! The point is not to make every instructional moment a level 3 or higher; rather, the goal is to become more intentional about your practice. By learning what high-quality inquiry practice entails, you will be more likely to implement it successfully when it is your desired instructional approach. And though I have downplayed the importance of leading at a level 3 (proficient inquiry) and higher rating for all lessons, I will say unequivocally that level 3 and 4 should be the target for a significant portion of instruction if improving student achievement is the goal.

7

How Do You Create a Successful, Well-Managed Inquiry Classroom?

One of the greatest fears for teachers is losing control—control of instruction, control of students, control of the class. Inquiry-based learning by necessity requires teachers to move from a controlling role to more of a facilitating role. Until teachers embrace this new role of facilitator, they will be unwilling to implement inquiry instruction and therefore unable to work to achieve the goal of working toward what is best for students. Management issues are the main reason that people leave the teaching profession (Barmby, 2006), so strong management skills are critical to a teacher's success.

I hear some teachers say, "Inquiry works with students of high ability but not students of lower ability, because of behavioral issues." But I also hear other teachers say, "Inquiry techniques work best with students of lower ability because inquiry provides a way to engage these students in learning, some for the first time." So why the contradiction?

I believe the contradiction found in teachers' receptivity to using inquiry instruction rests, at least in part, on their success (or lack thereof) in managing the classroom effectively. Classroom management is undoubtedly one of the most critical aspects associated with effective instruction and learning. Poor management can destroy any chance for meaningful learning. However, the converse is not necessarily true. Strong management is necessary for effective instruction, but it does not in and of itself ensure that powerful learning will follow.

Although managing student behavior may be the most obvious form of classroom management (and the one that breeds the most fear for teachers), other areas of classroom management deserve attention, too. The following sections will discuss factors that compose an effective, successful learning environment.

Projecting a Solid Presence

Any two teachers can say the same thing to a class yet be perceived differently. The distinction comes down to presence. A commanding presence comprises four essential qualities: firmness, fairness, confidence, and "with-it-ness." Although these qualities tend to improve with experience, novice teachers can still establish a presence that will quickly pass the test that their students will inevitably send their way.

To be clear, firmness is not meanness. As teachers, we should *never* be mean, but we do need to be firm. A teacher needs to be the adult in the room, set reasonable boundaries, and expect that everyone live within those boundaries.

Fairness does not mean equal treatment. Fairness strives for equity and impartiality; thus, successful teachers avoid playing favorites. Treating students with impartiality and equity means addressing the unique needs of each learner.

Confidence, not cockiness, is a self-assurance that gives you a comfortable manner. Possessing solid content knowledge is one great step in building confidence. There is no substitute for deeply knowing and understanding your content—study, read, and study some more. Knowledge means going far beyond memorization of concepts and extends to being able to apply the content to your students' everyday life and to other concepts they are learning. Confidence also includes a sense of knowing yourself, your strengths and limitations, and an acknowledgment that you care about your students and that you show that in your interactions with them.

With-it-ness is a global understanding of what is transpiring in the class at a given time. Such awareness develops when a teacher cares about her students, their learning, and the content that she teaches. With-it-ness is characterized by the teacher's ability to make the content, the learning, and the learners all seamlessly flow together.

Inspiring Respect

If all learners were the same, we could just plug in a video of an excellent teacher each day to do the teaching for us. Yet, we know that our students' needs, abilities, and goals are unique, so our profession requires us to develop a professional rapport with and an understanding of each student. Thus, our task as teachers includes facilitating the development of a caring and respectful learning environment.

A common mistake is to think that respect is given and earned in the same way. Respect is partially culturally dependent. In some settings, respect is yielded up front—you are respected until you lose it. In other settings, particularly those in which the teacher is not a member of the dominant culture, respect must be earned. Thus, if you lack cultural understanding of your setting, you will likely be frustrated when students do not bestow you with immediate respect (Marshall, 2008).

Even when respect takes more time to develop, you can still do several things to encourage that regard. The first step is to acknowledge any cultural differences and remain patient even when norms or belief systems differ from your own. Be honest with yourself and with the students: admit to the students that respect may take time, and commit to them that you are OK with that. In the meantime, however, let the students know that you have general expectations regarding decency and civility that everyone must follow. Students do not have to agree with everyone in the class, but you can expect that they will listen to each other, hear each other out, and find appropriate ways to dissent.

Holding High Expectations

Many classes that I have observed have no explicit expectations for students. The underlying principle is that the teacher will teach and students will learn, the students' effectiveness in mastering what is taught will determine their grades, and so it goes. Well, I typically do not see the happy ending, especially when so many students are failing. For teachers of classes with high pass rates, you are not off the hook, either; you owe it to your students to challenge them and help them increase their knowledge and improve their skills, both in the content area and in their process skills (e.g., problem solving, communicating evidence).

What do high, yet attainable, expectations have to do with classroom management? When expectations are clear and high, students know where they are going, see how their learning fits into the bigger picture, and tend to see a subject's relevance. Therefore, high expectations turn into a pattern that becomes a proactive means to manage student learning. When learning has purpose, behavior problems plummet and learning becomes the focal point.

Expectations can be cocreated with students. When students feel they have a voice, they are more likely to engage in learning and will even defend it when scoffed at by peers. One means of setting expectations is to have students set short- and long-term goals. Long-term goals may be about their performance in the course. Short-term goals may be as simple as having them outline what they will achieve today. Goal setting has become particularly popular in middle school settings and can help narrow the achievement gap. Having students focus on clear goals each day helps them organize and prioritize—two difficult things for many students. Encouraging students to set their own goals and determining collectively appropriate expectations create a venue that challenges students and minimizes boredom. Many troublemakers are not malicious—they are just bored. Yes, some of these students are also missing some critical content and skills, but discipline problems are most often a call for help and an avoidance of failure rather than a calculated attempt to sabotage your class.

 TIP Greatest Management Challenge

Which aspect of classroom management discussed thus far—establishing a solid presence, developing respectful relationships, or setting high expectations—presents the greatest challenge for you? Why? How will you improve this aspect of management?

Critical Elements of Inquiry Classrooms

Projecting a solid presence, encouraging respect, and setting high expectations are all helpful, proactive management strategies that work in inquiry-based classes. But some challenges inherent to inquiry-based teaching and learning call for additional approaches.

Setting Your Class Up for Success on Day 1

Unquestionably, day 1 is the best opportunity we have to establish the conditions that nurture an effective learning environment that supports inquiry-based learning. Within a few minutes, students are already making up their minds about whether they will enjoy coming to class, how much they are likely to gain from the class, and what effort they will be putting forth for the rest of the term. You can do a few specific things on day 1 to tilt the scales in your favor.

Engage Students. First—and I do mean as soon as possible—engage students in a short but meaningful learning experience, one that requires thought and effort but one for which they can experience success. This brief, early experience sets the stage for future inquiry experiences. Collaboration and engagement are necessary to inquiry-based learning that seeks to promote deep, critical thinking.

Avoid Policy Discussions. Granted, you may be required to address school policies on day 1, but, if possible, shy away from details on rules, policies, syllabi, and book checkouts. Remember, this kind of material is likely all they will hear or have heard all day long. All those topics are important, but they can be gradually addressed during the first week. Rules and policies, though important, can stifle energy and creativity, if present, so seek to engage students on the first day.

Create Learning Stations. Teachers who are required by their school to cover all the nuts and bolts on the first day of class can still use strategies for doing so that engage students in the process. One such strategy uses a series of learning stations for the first day. This approach reduces the focus on you on a day when nerves tend to be a little raw anyway. Learning stations provide great time management techniques for completing these otherwise mundane tasks. There is no reason for the entire class to watch while you pass out books one at a time.

An example of learning stations might include a series of 5- or 10-minute rotations where students would accomplish each of the following:

- Check out a text (have students take a book, sign the form that they received the book, record the number of the book, and find a few key things in the text).
- Complete an intriguing math problem.

- Take a short quiz to test competency (e.g., ask them to use a triple beam balance to measure the mass of two objects and record their answers to the hundredth of a gram).

- Pick up a copy of the syllabus and respond to a couple of key questions (e.g., "What should you do if you miss a day of class?").

- Complete a personal information sheet (name, contact numbers, e-mail address, parents' names and numbers, hobbies, and other general things you would like to know).

- Work in a team of two or three students (have a task that requires students to plan and work collaboratively, such as building the tallest free-standing tower using 1 foot of tape and 25 straws).

Try to provide a variety of tasks and materials at the various stations (e.g., logistics issues, content explorations, prior knowledge). You will need about 10 stations for a class of 30 students. The key to successful learning stations is to make them nearly equal in time to complete. If one station's task is particularly short, then add a brief problem for students to address. If students see the learning stations as a sort of scavenger hunt that provides clues to the upcoming year, it is easier to get buy-in from them.

Thinking, Doing, Exploring. For teachers who have some flexibility on day 1 requirements, save the learning stations for another day. Instead, get students thinking, doing, and exploring. Creating a feeling of success should be one of the primary goals for the first day of class. You may give them a challenging problem later, but students should not be concerned with failing on their first attempt in your class. Here are three specific suggestions:

- *Get students questioning* (e.g., "Come up with 10 questions that you have about the world around you"). It may not surprise you that students have a difficult time asking good questions. I give my preservice science teachers 15 minutes to go outside and write 20 good "scientific" questions that they have as they look around campus. Few ever come back with 20 questions. In math, ask students to come up with a list of questions about each other that they would like to know—information we can use later to tackle key standards, including data collection and analysis. This activity leads into a great discussion about asking good questions, and students quickly realize how difficult it can be to create a good question. Working collaboratively in small groups or as a class, students can experience success with creating good questions—something that may have been individually challenging.

- *Get students observing* (e.g., "Make 10 observations of things around the room"). An important clarification to make with students is the difference between observations and inferences. Observations are facts based on information received through one or more of the five senses (e.g., "The flower at the back of the room has five petals"). An inference is an interpretative statement (e.g., "The flower needs water because it is drooping").

- *Get students collecting data* (e.g., "Weigh 10 objects without a conventional scale"). Some examples of data-gathering activities include weighing, counting, classifying, organizing, finding dimensions, or measuring time. Collecting data also involves learning effective ways to organize the data. At first, a class discussion may be helpful to plan how to organize data, but as the school year progresses, students should become more self-sufficient.

Controlling the Degree of Change

As you lead inquiry-based lessons, remember that your students have not had all the same experiences that you have had – nor even the same experiences as their peers. Provide appropriate scaffolding to help your students transition to inquiry learning. Additionally, recognize that most people do not embrace change at first, so understand that your students make need time to acclimate to new ideas, new routines, and new ways of thinking.

The rubrics in Chapter 6 can help guide your increased proficiency relative to implementation of inquiry-based instruction. If your goal is to be at a level 3 for a given inquiry investigation but you are beginning at level 1, then build toward level 2, which tends to be more teacher directed and prescriptive than level 3. Nearly all commercial lessons are written at level 2. As students begin to assume more ownership in their learning (e.g., learning how to organize ideas, data, and their thinking in more self-directed and persistent ways), then the level of inquiry can be raised to match their new abilities. In other words, you are providing scaffolding not only for yourself but for your students as well.

Even if you are already at level 2, keep in mind that inquiry will be new for many students, so you will still need to provide transitional experiences for them. Beginning the year with level 3 instruction would likely cause undue frustration and ultimately resentment and behavioral problems.

Fostering Cooperative Learning

One of the qualities that often distinguishes inquiry-based forms of learning from other approaches is the degree of interaction that it entails. Though inquiry can be done in isolation, learning is often social and better accomplished with cooperative forms of learning. This opportunity to increase knowledge through interpersonal interactions can also present a great challenge. Namely, how do you facilitate such learning without the classroom slipping into utter chaos?

First, realize that student discussion can be a good thing. If silence is your modus operandi, you might want to rethink why silence is so important to you and what you believe it achieves. Compliance and silence do not mean that any learning is occurring—they only ensure that disruptions are minimized. Since silence does not equate to learning, the trick is to make sure that talk is directed positively toward the topic of focus. A second consideration is the size of small groups in your classroom and the nature of their work.

Determine Group Size. When you ask students to work together, determine the group size—whether pairs or larger groups—based on your objectives and the capacity to engage everyone in the group. At times, supplies will dictate the minimum group size. When greater flexibility is possible, I have had the best results when groups contain two to three students. In mathematics, pairs of students are often appropriate if communication of process is the target. Students can alternate writing detailed solutions on handheld whiteboards, for example, and strategies such as think-pair-share can be readily employed. However, groups of three can also work well, particularly when resources are limited. Once groups get larger than three, there is a tendency for "tagalongs" who are not explicitly involved.

Regardless of the small-group size, classroom management requires that you keep things moving at a pace that is brisk enough to promote a sense of urgency but slow enough to allow students time to think.

Creating this sense of urgency will be discussed more in the section on time usage.

Different strategies, of course, work better for different teachers, but I encourage you to reassign groups frequently. In math, you may want to change groups every three weeks or so, but in science classes, I encourage reassigning groups every six to nine weeks because the investigations tend to be a bit longer and supply issues tend to be more complicated. Inevitably, students will be assigned to work with classmates they do not like, but assure them that this arrangement is only temporary, reminding them that they can (and must) get along.

Assess Individual Accountability in Group Work. Regardless of the group size, it is vital that individual accountability is weighted more heavily than group performance in the final grade for a project or investigation. Many rubrics are available to help with distributing the credit appropriately (Marshall, 2006). Giving appropriate credit allows students to work as teams but requires individuals to be responsible for knowing and understanding. I encourage students to explore and discuss together, but then provide individual explanations, conclusions, or summaries of the group's findings. Facilitating group work that has individual accountability is a proactive means to addressing parent and student concerns about unequal workload receiving similar credit. Students will also benefit by fully understanding the criteria by which they will be assessed and thus will become more focused on the work at hand (Mergendoller, Markham, Ravitz, & Larmer, 2006).

So if the grade earned is backed by individual accountability, why should students want to cooperate with group members? Perhaps you can provide an incentive for groups to encourage the success of all members on a given objective. A positive incentive (e.g., verbal encouragement or a percentage of a group grade) encourages peer tutoring, group reviews, and a team atmosphere. Also, if the task is appropriate and challenging enough, students will know that it is difficult, if not impossible, to achieve success in isolation and will thus *want* to work together (Lotan, 2006). Examples of good group activities include building a mousetrap racer (see Chapter 5, pp. 68–77) or solving a math problem that requires at least three different approaches. By rotating the groups regularly, you also lessen the concerns that a student might have for being stuck with someone who seems not to care or doesn't want to contribute.

Undoubtedly, issues will come up, such as the student who does not want to do anything or, at the other extreme, the student who wants to take over and do everything. In the first case, if students are not performing at all in the group, have them complete the assignment alone—with the hope that they realize it is easier and more productive to work in a team. Sometimes students want to be removed from a group so that they do not have to overcome shyness or social awkwardness. The goal with these students should be to get them back into a group as soon as possible and assign them a specific role that helps them focus. For students who tend to dominate groups, address the issue quickly and privately, away from their peers. Giving students specific roles can also help reduce this issue (roles may include data recorder or materials person).

Be creative! Allow students to channel Donald Trump on *Celebrity Apprentice* and "fire" group members for a day if they do not meet a deadline or fall short of previously stated expectations.

 ## TIP   Cooperative Learning

What obstacle needs to be removed or lessened for cooperative learning to thrive in your classroom? What are some possible solutions? What specific strategies can you apply to your next lesson? How would you respond to parents who say that their child did the majority of the group project and that the extra work, expectations, and grade are not fair?

Asking the Right Questions

The type of questions you ask directly relates to your expectations of students. Ask students questions that challenge them to think deeply. If the class has reached a point in the lesson where students do not know answers, then let them conduct some research before they engage in the discourse. For example, asking students to discuss what they can do to influence global warming will generate rich discussion and deep thinking. Contrast this with questions such as "What did you get for problem 5?" Questions that lead to one-word responses do not generate meaningful discourse.

When reviewing problem sets, post the solutions on the board or overhead and then ask students which problems they found difficult or confusing, and why. Then focus the discussion on clarifying both process issues and concepts. The goal is to improve thinking in areas where the greatest challenges exist, not just to treat everything as equal and lower level. The section on Discourse indicators in the EQUIP protocol in Chapter 6 (p. 100) discusses additional things to consider when leading questioning and discussion in an inquiry classroom.

Employing wait time and having all students engaged in the discourse are critical aspects of successful instruction that, with practice, every teacher can do. When you ask a question, wait for about five seconds (which will seem like five minutes if you have not practiced this before) and then call on someone (Rowe, 1987). The amount of wait time depends on the complexity of the question. If you call on a student before you ask the question, most of the rest of the class will disengage. (The only time I would suggest calling on a student first is when you are subtly trying to bring that student's attention back to the class—a non-disruptive form of behavior management.) Do not let the student off the hook with a response like "I don't know," but continue probing, perhaps reducing the depth of your question before following up further. If a student shows true resistance in answering a question, do not try to resolve the issue in front of the class; do it at another time, and try to get the student back on track the next day.

A second form of wait time is also beneficial. After a student responds, allow the other students time to think and react before you respond (Tobin, 1987). This technique encourages whole-class discussion instead of a teacher-student dialogue.

Many teachers are far too quick to say something like "That's right" or "No." Don't steal from the students the obligation and opportunity to think for themselves; instead, lead them so that they can determine the soundness of their own reasoning. Indeed, sometimes you should answer questions directly or comment on students' responses, but your first reaction should be to answer questions with questions and draw reactions from the class.

When students ask you a question, you quickly need to decide whether you are going to answer it directly, let another student answer it, or respond with another question. I encourage directly answering a question when a student seems excessively frustrated or asks a procedural question that doesn't directly involve the concept. If it is something that other students should know or are curious about, encourage them to respond to the question. Finally, when the student question is about the concept or problem at hand, it is appropriate to redirect the question back to the student. For instance, if a student says, "I don't understand how to solve this," an effective response is to get the student to articulate what he does or does not know. You might say, "Explain how you've tried to solve the problem and where you seem to be getting stuck." This response encourages students to be metacognitive about their own learning instead of relying on you to rescue them. By learning to take this step, they will become more independent in their learning.

If you feel that many students are struggling with the same question, then have everyone talk in a small groups for 30 seconds to determine the answer. Then ask the question again, either directed toward the original student or the whole class.

TIP Meaningful Conversations

How can you get students talking more and thinking deeper about core ideas and major concepts? How can you modify your questioning techniques to achieve this? What are the three most important questions to ask your students in tomorrow's lesson?

Keeping an Appropriate Pace

Learning takes time, so we need to give students sufficient opportunities to reflect on new ideas. However, this point does not negate the importance of judicially using and managing time. So how do we determine how to best allocate the time to facilitate the greatest growth in our students? Three specific aspects of classroom management help guide the pace of instruction: flow, transitions, and time usage. Also, because games are an important aspect of instruction in many classes, I address their role in the pace of a classroom.

Flow. Flow is established when high expectations fit within students' aptitude. Flow is confirmed when students comment that class "flew by"—proof they were deeply engaged.

Transitions. Part of keeping a class moving and focused on learning is to make sure that transitions are quick and appear seamless. Students need to know exactly what to do next, and there should be a sense of immediacy. If papers are to be turned in, establish a routine for doing so. For instance, a teacher might say, "Please pass your papers forward." The routine may be that students pass all papers forward in a row, then to the right until one student has them all. That student is responsible for placing the papers in the appropriate box.

As you transition from a lab investigation to a class discussion, students should know where they are supposed to be, what they should have ready, and when the next portion of the lesson will begin. For example, as groups are finishing data collection, provide a cue that students have five minutes to finish working on the lab. At the end of five minutes, students are expected to be in their seats, ready to take notes and engage in class discussion. Provide the cue again with two minutes remaining and then again with one minute remaining. A cue sequence provides clear expectations as it allows students time to get to a good stopping point.

The amount of time required to transition depends on the two portions of the lesson being bridged. When lots of materials and tasks are involved, then the transitions are typically longer. Regardless, be clear and follow through consistently.

If the class is struggling with transitions, practice them. "We are now going to practice moving your chairs from being in groups to being ready for a class discussion. We will do this several times until [list the problem] is resolved. I will wait until everyone is completely settled before we transition again." This rehearsal may seem like a waste of class time, but if you resolve this management matter in 10 minutes with a little practice, then you may have solved an issue that could steal several minutes at each transition all year.

TIP Lesson Transitions

What are three ways to improve transitions during your next lesson? How are students likely to respond to these changes? What will allow you to succeed, and what may hinder you?

Time Usage. Closely tied to transitions and flow is time usage. With many middle schools and high schools now on block schedules where students are in one class for 90 minutes, using time wisely is imperative to maximize learning. Using time wisely does not mean just doing more of the same—which for many teachers is to lecture, model the expected solution method, and then provide time for guided practice. Doubling these practices from what occurred in the 45-minute class period does not reflect the new opportunities intended and provided for in the block schedule. For starters, instruction needs to include strategies that actively engage the learner for a significant portion of class time. Staying the course of lecture longer, model longer, and complete more practice problems is neither effective nor efficient time use and leads to greater boredom and disengaged students. It is also contrary to the inquiry-based practices being advocated in this book.

As you plan, keep in mind that people can typically concentrate for about 10 to 20 minutes before beginning to zone out, particularly if they are sedentary and are functioning merely as recipients of knowledge. Break or chunk your class into segments; the components of the 4E × 2 Instructional Model can serve as a guide. For example, a lesson could begin with a quick 10- to 15-minute Engage that provides some formative data about students' prior knowledge on the topic—say, genetic inheritance. Perhaps use a KWHL chart, a formative probe, or a brainstorming session based on essential questions: "How do you get your hair color? Do we inherit personalities?" Without resolving students' misconceptions at this point, have students explore traits and diseases that we inherit and the process responsible for inherited traits. This Explore phase would likely take the remainder of a typical class period to finish, so it should be broken into specific and targeted pieces. For instance, you could suggest this activity: "For the next 20 minutes, your team is to use the following resources to help discover how we inherit traits. Discuss as a group, but record your findings individually." If appropriate, follow up this work with more exploration, assigning more tasks to complete: "Your team will have to use visuals and share with the class how you believe inheritance of certain traits occurs." Alternatively, you could bring the entire class back to synthesize their results before you challenge them with another task.

When you need to reinforce a major concept (which should be often), break the lesson into chunks that all support the same concept. For example, for a 55-minute class period, ask students to work on a problem in a small team (5 minutes), discuss solutions and their process including various solution methods (10 minutes), solve a slightly easier yet related problem individually (5 minutes), discuss challenges and questions (8 minutes), solve a new extension or twist in groups (5 minutes), discuss their solutions (5 minutes), clarify and summarize (5 minutes), take a two-question quiz that emphasizes the process and the key concept (12 minutes). This is an example of a lesson that transitions often while trying to make sure that no one is ever frustrated for more than five minutes at a time. It also provides opportunities for you to work with teams and individuals throughout the class. Notice that the class time is not spent just showing a solution. Instead, it is about process—how did students solve the problem, where did they struggle, and what are some alternate solutions?

Games. Games to review or practice after a concept has been learned can be a great motivator. From a classroom management standpoint, two questions should be paramount in your decision to use a particular game: (1) Does the time spent learning and reviewing content far exceed the time spent on nonlearning activities such as explaining rules and scoring? (2) Are both content and process skills emphasized in the game? If the answer to either of these is no, then you might reconsider whether to use the game.

One of the most common games played in the classroom is Jeopardy. While I am a fan of the game in general, in many cases too much time is spent arguing over rules, points, whose turn it is, and what topic and point value should be selected next. None of those things has anything to do with learning. In other, more efficient scenarios, the focus is on memorization rather than deeper understanding. So find a game you like and then modify it until you are satisfied that it serves the purpose of being highly engaging and focused on learning. The list of possibilities is nearly endless—Trivial Pursuit, Password, Twenty Questions, Horse Race, Baseball, Family Feud, and Are You Smarter Than a 5th Grader. Adapt them to your purpose, but keep it focused and moving quickly. Also remember everything does not have to be a contest—devise a game in which everyone can win.

When you use a game in your class, find a way to make most of the points come toward the end of the game. Students are more likely to stay engaged because they have a chance to score until the end. Also keep in mind that not all students enjoy competition, so make the game one where everyone can have success. For instance, suggest, "If your team scores more than X points, everyone in the group will receive 2 points toward your test grade." Even better, have a few questions at the conclusion of the game for students to answer individually on paper.

Points for these questions can be added to the team score to give an overall individual score. Finally, to maximize class time, do not take time to record individual results during class. Collect the papers, score them (which will tell you how well students individually know the major ideas), and hand them back with their total score the next day.

Addressing Immaturity of Students

Some teachers lament that their students are just too immature for inquiry. In some settings, students deemed at risk are also denied inquiry-based instruction because teachers fear behavioral problems. Although it is true that some students are more adept at working in groups than others, this should not change your responsibility as a teacher to provide the richest learning experience possible for all students. In fact, students deemed too immature or at risk are often the ones who benefit the most from inquiry-based instruction.

For example, I worked with at-risk students in a dropout recovery program who were considered disruptive and too immature for "normal" classroom instruction. Instead of teaching physics and communication skills in a traditional way, I drew on their interests and experience with automobiles, electronics, and welding to create a solar-powered vehicle that was eventually raced in a national competition. Students who needed communications credit worked on a team that designed, practiced, and then gave presentations to executives at major corporations to raise money for the project. In the third year, the project resulted in a vehicle that won two national competitions (a 62-mile track race and a three-day trans-state race), and then the students used the vehicle to compete against other schools, engineers, and corporations in an international solar vehicle race in Japan (Marshall, 2004). For a teacher, there is nothing more exciting than to see students succeeding in amazing ways, including being honored by the governor, after being told year after year that they were failures. Maybe the previous failure was the education system—not the students.

Your story doesn't have to be on the same scale to be just as meaningful. The point is that all students are entitled to great instruction, even if that means a little extra work or scaffolding. Find out their interests and build inquiry-based experiences that focus on these interests. Have them determine questions that they want to investigate. Often, the real challenge is not that the students are immature or at risk, but that they do not see a purpose or have interest in what we are asking them to do. Connecting science, mathematics, engineering, and technology to their world can make a huge impact. Students will engage when their curiosity and interest have been piqued; their energy will be directed in a positive direction rather than in a manner that disrupts learning for everyone.

TIP Student Maturity

As expectations and rigor increase for students, how can you help improve student maturity during the year to promote greater success toward your learning goals?

Bridging Gaps in Language Skills

When language and communication skills are poor, inquiry can provide a means to engage the learner and to help him bridge the deficits. Students with poor language skills may be either native or nonnative English speakers—the way the teacher addresses students' underdeveloped language skills is nearly identical. Regardless of the reason, the student does not have the skills to read, write, or communicate on grade level. English Language Learners (ELLs) or English as a Second Language (ESL) students who speak little or no English often face the greatest challenge in our classes because they often lack both the written and oral skills necessary to understand and communicate their knowledge. We have options as to how we respond. We can seek to engage language learners as meaningfully as possible, or we can choose to ignore them and just help them slide through the system on the path of least resistance. The former option means that we need to get them in groups listening, observing, and interacting to the best of their ability. On your end as a teacher, it means providing diagrams, visuals, and abbreviated notes to assist students as they make sense out of a new world. Remember that although ESL students may be fluent in their first language, you are expecting them to learn a new language and grow their vocabulary at the same time that they are learning important new content. Having these students work in inquiry-based settings with other students will give them far more opportunities to interact with the content than they will get from listening to a lecture.

Labs in science or problem-solving sessions in math that involve manipulatives can be extremely helpful for ELL students because they can observe the world or mathematical phenomenon (i.e., in algebra or statistics) without needing language. However, the degree to which the students make sense of the experience will depend on the support that you can offer, their prior knowledge in the subject area, and any assistance that can be provided by peers.

Debate surrounds the question of whether you should try to communicate with ESL students in their native language, but the general consensus seems to be that working with ESL students in English helps them make the transition more quickly. That said, greeting the student or exchanging a few pleasantries in the student's native tongue is a good way to build rapport and show you care.

Engaging Honors Students

I have found that leading inquiry with honors students can be enjoyable, rewarding, and challenging. When students see the value in the inquiry experience, they reap the benefits. However, honors students have mastered the game of school. By introducing inquiry to these students, you may be seen as a danger to their success because you are changing the rules to the game. Now you are requiring them to think, analyze, and question, which may lead to some resistance and frustration.

In most cases, you can help honors students work through these fears by showing them that inquiry promotes critical thinking, something that is essential for success in college and in their future careers. Furthermore, inquiry promotes lifelong learning and allows them to pursue individual interests and desires to learn more about something and then to begin a quest to grow in that area. Finally, you can create increased buy-in from individuals in this group if you can assure them that with some work on their end, you will help guide them toward success in inquiry learning as well as real life.

Experiences with inquiry-based teaching may be the first time that some of these honors students have been challenged to think deeply. Many have mastered memorizing algorithms and following procedures, so the challenge can also reengage those who are academically gifted but bored with the current system. Nevertheless, you should expect initial reluctance on their part and comments like "Just tell me what to do."

Perhaps the most important thing you can do is to make sure that your summative assessments (those that count for grades) are fully aligned with your instruction. If you teach for understanding but test only algorithms and facts that your students have memorized, students will quickly learn that the inquiry-based processes are not important. However, if your assessments expect students to create, apply, analyze, and engage in other high-order processes, they will quickly learn that these skills are critical to their success—and honors students value their success.

General Elements of Well-Managed Classrooms

Some qualities of sound classroom management apply to any classroom, not just inquiry-focused ones. No matter what your preferred instructional practice, all teachers should strive for a classroom with appropriate routines, rules, and technology and fair discipline plans and reward systems.

Routines

Routines are especially beneficial when working with students with special needs, but all students benefit from knowing how to come into class, where to submit assignments, what to do as they finish lab investigations, how to work safely in a lab setting, or how to work effectively in teams. Do your students know when you are ready to begin class or when it is time to move on without you saying a word? Is there a bell, a place you stand, a timer that counts down, or a light flash that lets students know when you are ready to begin? The cue may be verbal as well, such as a "Good morning," but the point is you need a consistent behavior to let students know that you are ready to begin. If your class starts with a warm-up activity, students should know that they are to come in, see the warm-up on the board, and be working by the time that the final bell sounds.

"Dead time" can often lead to disruptions. Because students work at different speeds, they will finish assignments at different times. You can avoid dead time in various ways. Many problems or investigations can be solved at multiple levels. You can set a minimum level that all students need to achieve, and then provide additional challenging levels for those who finish early, thus also delivering differentiated instruction. You can also use a set of challenge problems that rotate every few weeks. Set a minimum number that all students must complete during a grading period and expect students to work on these when they have completed their regular assignments (or tests or quizzes); the key is to make sure that students have something meaningful to do.

Rules

As adults, we work under a set of assumed rules and guidelines, but as students are growing and developing, establishing and communicating a common set of principles to guide interactions is important. I recommend having or cocreating with students a short set of rules—no more than five rules. If facilitated well, having students participate in the democratic process of determining rules will likely generate the same rules as you would supply, but it has the advantage of giving students a voice in the classroom.

Grandmount (2003) has suggested the following global set of rules:

1. Act in a safe and healthy way.
2. Treat all property with respect.
3. Respect the rights and needs of others.
4. Take responsibility for learning.

Remember that a rule is only beneficial if you are willing to enforce it. You must enforce rules consistently. It's human nature to push boundaries from time to time, but one sure recipe for disaster is to be inconsistent in applying rules. To go weeks ignoring a rule and then suddenly begin enforcing it will make students angry and rebellious.

Safety. Regardless of the specific rules and expectations in your classroom, there is one nonnegotiable: *learning must be done safely*. Although accidents can and will happen in any classroom, doing what you can to ensure that students are learning in a safe manner, in a safe environment, is critical. Safety is especially critical in laboratory science classes.

Safety begins by using materials and equipment—including classroom desks and pencils—as they were intended to be used, storing and handling chemicals properly, making sure to review safety issues with students before they begin, and cleaning up properly after finishing an activity. In an inquiry setting where students may be engaged in related but different investigations simultaneously, it is important that you approve all procedures before groups begin their exploration. Set clear consequences when teams deviate from a procedure without your approval so that you are aware of what students are doing, yet they are given reasonable freedom to explore in unique ways.

Security. Unfortunately, some students may be tempted to steal equipment, so it is important to have an efficient, quick means to make sure everything is accounted for before class is dismissed. Once an item leaves the classroom, it is nearly impossible to recover it.

For calculators, a box with a slot for each one or a hanging holder with clear pouches (some teachers use hanging shoe organizers) will allow you to quickly scan to confirm that all are returned before you dismiss class. Electronic balances are particularly popular, so either lock them down or do a quick inventory before ending the class. A check-out policy—similar to books—may work for classrooms in which students need frequent access to items such as glassware, computers, calculators, or other tools, but only if they can lock the items away in individual drawers or lockers.

PowerPoint and Student Learning

Technology, when used properly, has much to offer in an inquiry-based learning environment. One of the most frequently used forms of technology in the classroom is a PowerPoint presentation. When PowerPoint and its newer cousin, Prezi, were first brought into classrooms, it was captivating because it was flashy and novel. The novelty has largely worn off, but the flash still often overshadows a true demonstration of content. For student presentations, make sure that your assessment rubrics are largely about clarity, knowledge, and depth of thought, not about the colorful graphics.

PowerPoint allows teachers to plow through massive amounts of material without necessarily achieving clear understanding among students. I suggest that PowerPoint notes, in general, not exceed 15 minutes of class. Realize that students typically tune out after 15 to 20 minutes (less for elementary students), but we often hold them responsible for the material given during longer lectures. Consequently, notes should be interspersed with opportunities for students to engage in the material and ask question. For instance, after five minutes of notes (two to three slides), have students turn to their neighbor and discuss the key points and determine what they are still confused about. Quick discussions give an interactive component to notetaking and provide you with quick feedback as to where students are still struggling.

Technology in different forms encourages and allows students to interact with key concepts, such as scientific and graphing calculators, probes (e.g., motion detectors, light detectors), and interactive software applications. One of the great advantages of technology is that large amounts of data can be gathered and analyzed rapidly. The challenge is to make sure that the technology becomes background and the content being studied becomes foreground. Technology becomes an impediment to learning when computers take too long to boot up, the learning curve is too long, the use of the software is unintuitive, the hardware and software are unstable and crash often, and students are overly distracted by the "wiz-bang-wow" of the technology. Remember that when technology is ineffective, it opens up another opportunity for behavioral problems and management issues.

• Begin class with computers up and running. Students can set up computers before the tardy bells rings and begin a warm-up activity while booting up.

• Reflect carefully on the learning objective and then seek out the best manner to achieve the objective. It may be more effective to just use paper and pencil, or another program may be much more user-friendly and can save time.

• Always check URLs the morning they will be used in the classroom. If your school has blocked the sites or if the Internet is too slow, then students will quickly become frustrated and disruptive. One solution may be to make some hard copies of several of the sites for groups to use. Remember to copy only the most critical sites that provide the content that students must have to succeed. When the Internet is functional, students can go to other sites that may be more interactive or contain video. Another option is to partially download web pages to computers so that they are available when the computers are offline.

A final management tip: position yourself so that you can see most of the computer screens with a quick glance. If students typically face the front of the class, then you may wish to be in the back. This tip is applicable to solid classroom management and to inquiry-based instruction. As you circulate through the room to monitor individuals or groups, position yourself so that you can see the majority of students. Getting down to students' eye level is important for rapport, and positioning yourself properly is important to be able to see what is going on throughout the classroom.

Discipline Plan

Even in the most proactive, well-managed class, misbehavior will occur. Then what? First, realize that a student's misbehavior usually has one of four causes: seeking attention, seeking power, seeking revenge, or seeking isolation (Dreikers, Pepper, & Grunwald, 1998). Sometimes misbehavior results from a combination of these root causes. For instance, students who refuse to turn in any work and seem intent on failing the course may be seeking power and revenge. The revenge may be to get back at parents who have hurt them emotionally. Students quickly realize that grades are one of the few areas where they actually have almost complete control. They can choose to fail or choose to succeed, but no one can force students to achieve.

Many schools have a discipline plan, but any plan should include a series of steps that advance depending on the severity and frequency of the behavior. Behavioral interventions fall along a continuum from low to extensive: extinction (i.e., ignoring the problem), nonverbal desists, verbal desists, reprimands, time-outs, and severe punishment that ultimately could end in suspension or expulsion from the school (Cruickshank, Jenkins, & Metcalf, 2006).

Be sure to think through your consequences and ensure that they match the school's policy. If you do have cumulative consequences (e.g., for the first violation, you warn the student; for the second violation, the student comes in after class), make sure you know when things start over. Is each class period a fresh start? Each week? Each quarter? Whatever you decide should be clear and logical to both you and your students.

If the behavior is more of an annoyance and you know the student is seeking attention, then begin with extinction, or ignoring the behavior. Find a good time to give positive attention by catching the student in an appropriate moment that can be praised. Your main purpose with extinction is to prevent the student from receiving reinforcement for the annoying behavior, so do not ignore the behavior if the student is getting some type of reinforcement from others or, of course, if the behavior persists.

When behavior surpasses minor annoyances, action is needed. In most cases, the "evil eye" is enough of a nonverbal desist to stop the behavior with minimal to no interruption of instructional time. Being successful with this technique relates directly to the presence you have established in the class. Sometimes a sharp glance does not work, leading to the next levels of intervention, which are often the most troubling to teachers. These infractions involve an ongoing disturbance that, when multiplied by several students, can effectively stop classroom instruction.

A structured discipline plan like the one just described goes a long way to minimize disruptive behaviors, but when the need arises to squelch minor disturbances, use interventions that are timely, personal, appropriate, and future focused. *Timely* means that the intervention should happen immediately following the infraction or as soon possible. Often the next-best time is at the end of class, but definitely before the beginning of the next class, or during group. Your goal is to avoid embarrassing students in front of their peers, a situation that almost always backfires.

When we know what students really care about, we can begin to plan appropriate interventions. For instance, if playing on the basketball team is the most important thing to the student, then use this fact as leverage when needed. Have a private conversation to let the student know that her behavior is unacceptable and what the consequences will be if the misbehavior continues—missing practice and spending time in detention, meeting with the coach, and so forth. The last thing that you want to do is totally remove basketball from the student's school life because her love of basketball likely motivates her to stay in school.

Remember: don't threaten if you are not willing to follow through if the misbehavior occurs again. Also, corrective actions should be directed toward an individual and not an entire group, unless the issue is so widespread that you cannot distinguish the individuals involved. (If this happens often, improve the way that you monitor the class.) Also make sure the consequences are appropriate for the behavior. There is no need to suspend a student for two days for not turning in homework for two consecutive days.

Finally, keep the future in mind. When the dust has cleared, remember that in 99.9 percent of the cases, you will be working with this student for the remainder of the year, so think about building a win-win. You win when the students comply with your needs. The students win when they succeed in your class and have not been embarrassed in the process.

Reward System

We can easily get lost in the punishment side of things and forget the more powerful results that come from using rewards. Much has been written about the merits of intrinsic and extrinsic motivation (Kohn, 1993). Extrinsic rewards lead to short-term motivation, and intrinsic rewards are valuable for encouraging long-term motivation, which, in turn, leads to lifelong learning. I prefer intrinsic rewards (e.g., the satisfaction and confidence that are derived from success) over extrinsic rewards when possible, but most early schooling is built around an extrinsic reward system (e.g., grades, candy, physical awards). In other words, efforts to use intrinsic rewards will likely come up against some strong resistance.

Regardless of the reward structure you use, be careful to award academic credit only for academic learning. Many schools have instituted policies that underscore this practice, but I still see students getting points added to their grade for tasks like bringing cans to the school food drive. The cause is excellent, but it is not an academic activity.

8

Planning for Success: What Are the Meaningful Steps Forward?

In Chapter 1, I asked you to think about the teaching philosophy that undergirds your teaching, the practices that guide it, and the actions that facilitate learning. Now it's my turn. To me, it is critical to provide a learning environment that challenges all, engages all, and develops all to their fullest potential. This means *doing* science and math and communicating ideas through rigorous individual and group experiences. To make my philosophy a reality, I must know where students begin relative to targeted skills and knowledge. Then I must identify which approaches will appropriately challenge students so that they continue to grow and develop toward mastering the goals, national and state standards, and objectives held for them.

An especially important part of my philosophy is the emphasis on having students *do* science and math. A significant portion of all students' classroom science experiences, I believe, should entail doing science—not being told about science and then verifying a law or concept through a confirmatory activity later. The same holds true for mathematics: students should engage in doing mathematics and not just memorize procedures and algorithms.

Though your philosophy may differ from mine, you also desire to challenge all your students and to succeed with all your students. Success entails seeking solutions and avoiding the temptation to justify why inquiry-based instruction cannot possibly work in your classroom with your students. I know of nothing that will solve all the challenges we face in educating our students. However, inquiry teaching offers concrete steps that, when done well, will likely result in greater student achievement in both content knowledge and process skills.

TIP Future Steps

You have been asked to reflect on your educational philosophies, discuss current classroom practices, read examples of inquiry-based instruction, and analyze what makes one lesson more or less successful than another. Now it is time to ask, Where do you still need to grow? What aspects of your instruction are keeping you from thriving in your classroom and maximizing your students' achievement? These areas are now the targets for your professional development plan.

For most of us, transformation of practice involves a series of interrelated stages. These stages are dynamic—meaning that since we all come with different experiences, preparation, and knowledge, a one-size-fits-all approach is not realistic. The teachers within given schools or districts, however, often possess a common set of general strengths and weaknesses. Thus, in the following sections, I suggest how you might transform the quality of inquiry-based instruction being led by you, your team, or your school. No matter where you start, strive to master a few of your greatest challenges before forging ahead. Moving too quickly will likely yield poor results and frustration. Be sure to stop and celebrate even small improvements. When linked together, multiple small wins begin to bring about major improvements.

Pre-inquiry Stage

Those educators at the novice or pre-inquiry stage have heard about inquiry-based instruction but are not certain how to proceed with major components such as planning or implementation. The previous chapters should have been helpful in articulating the value and need along with the basic mechanisms tied to inquiry-based instruction. The recommendations that follow are all critical aspects in the development process.

Management Assessment

Effective management and thoughtfully organized teaching are necessary but not sufficient for exemplary inquiry-based teaching. Without effective management, the house of cards tumbles and learning flounders, at best; with effective management, the foundation is set to allow successful teaching and learning.

Review the major issues presented in Chapter 7, and then identify two or three management challenges that currently or likely would prevent you from moving forward with inquiry-based instruction. If the academic year is in progress, then slowly and purposefully address the issues in your classroom. For example, do you struggle with getting students to refocus after you transition from an activity back to a whole-class conversation? Have you thought through how to facilitate effective collaborative learning? Remember that changes need to be done incrementally to allow students time to adjust to new routines or expectations. To come in and radically increase the rigor of the classroom discourse, change to more student-centered learning, and raise expectations for students without providing sufficient scaffolding will be met with resistance, resentment, and, ultimately, failure.

Lesson Study

Chapters 4 and 5 offer examples of inquiry-based mathematics and science lessons that serve as good models. Additionally, you can visit the Inquiry in Motion website and log in (www.clemson.edu/iim/lessonplans) to access dozens of inquiry-based lessons—all free of charge.

Find a lesson from one of these or other resources that involves a topic that you teach. Read it closely and then analyze how it might work in your classroom. Ask yourself the following questions:

- Is this lesson developmentally appropriate for my students?
- Do my students have the prerequisite knowledge to allow them to succeed?
- How would I need to scaffold learning, if at all, so that my students will be challenged yet also successful?
- What modifications will I need to make based on prior teaching and student learning in my class?

Finally, remember the all-important tip for inquiry-focused teaching: do not fully explain the core concepts to students before they have time to meaningfully explore the concept themselves.

Start Small

Begin by adding one solid inquiry-based lesson to your curriculum each quarter. As your effectiveness increases, work to increase the percentage of time or number of lessons devoted to level 3 forms of inquiry (see Chapter 6).

Just as you are starting small by adding one inquiry-focused lesson each academic quarter, also start small from your students' perspective. Thus, the first experience may be a brief lesson (or one with significant scaffolds) to ensure that no student will be frustrated or overwhelmed for more than five minutes at a time. Part of learning involves becoming more comfortable with not immediately knowing the answer, but also having the skill set to know how to begin tackling complex and meaningful problems.

The Developing Stage

Those in the developing (or "the honeymoon is over") stage believe in and understand the basic premises associated with inquiry-based instruction but often lack the basic know-how for consistent, successful implementation in terms of management, planning, assessments, and so forth. Teachers at the developing stage frequently say that they have tried to lead inquiry in their classroom but feel that their students are not capable of learning that way. Additionally, teachers at this stage may not understand how students can explore concepts and ideas before explanation occurs.

Stop the Blame Game

Before you can transform your practice, you must realize the incredible influence that you have over your students' successes. Your influence can be good and bad. When your plan works, you celebrate. When it doesn't, you likely pass the buck. The first step is to quit blaming students. For one reason or another, students may not be excelling in your classroom. A myriad of factors could be responsible, such as too many changes for students based on prior experience, abrupt changes from what is familiar, or increased expectations without appropriate support to achieve the new goals.

Identify a current issue in your classroom (e.g., poor student engagement, low student achievement), and then begin to devise solutions to remedy it. Building solid relationships is a great first step. When your students see learning as a team effort, not a battle pitched between them and you, then they are willing to work harder and persist longer.

Assessing Success

If students are not fully prepared at test time, then think about ways to correct this before the test without sacrificing rigor or expectations. If 50 percent of the class is failing, this is a lose-lose situation: you undoubtedly feel horrible, and your students largely have not achieved the goals. Checking in regularly with students with short diagnostic (before beginning instruction) or formative (during instruction) assessments can help you and your students realize where they are prepared and where they still need work.

The actual number is not an absolute, but check in with (assess) your students in some way at least three times each class period. If three assessments in a period seem high, then you are not checking in enough. After every few minutes of notes or discussion, ask your students to record in their notebooks an answer to a question pertaining to the information—this practice encourages more active note taking and involvement in discussions. To focus and review at the beginning of class, pose a series of questions from previous lessons at various cognitive levels; have students respond to one another as if the listener were absent the previous day. Ask students to solve problems, analyze data sets, or interpret graphs with the student next to them; have one student record the thoughts, solution, or analysis provided by the other student. During all of these quick formative checks, you should be circulating around the room to look for misconceptions that need clarification, check for understanding, and consider new ways to address confusing areas.

Explore Before Explain

You likely have several lessons that have the potential to be solid inquiry lessons but need some revising. Start with what you deem to be a fairly successful lesson by your own standards, and then rework the lesson into a level 3 (Proficient Inquiry) lesson as described in Chapter 6.

One of the most critical aspects of effective inquiry-based instruction is allowing students to explore concepts in meaningful ways before you or your students provide explanations. This is a paradigm shift from how most teachers learned, yet the old method is analogous to delivering the punch line of the joke before telling the joke itself. Although sometimes it is appropriate and necessary to provide confirmatory or prescriptive forms of learning (e.g., demonstrating how to use a microscope), our natural curiosity of the world is fueled by exploring things before they are explained to us.

Please don't construe this recommendation to mean you can turn students loose to do whatever they choose. You have standards to help focus the learning. The foundation of your instruction should be based on the Common Core for State Standards in Mathematics and the Next Generation Science Standards, or some derivative of these (Achieve, 2013; National Governors Association Center for Best Practices & Council of Chief State School Officers, 2010). Initially, you will need additional thought and time to switch from a "tell first and then confirm" to an "Explore first and then Explain" approach, but when successfully facilitated, the payoff in terms of student achievement is wonderful.

Here's one way to create an Explore-before-Explain inquiry-focused lesson:

1. Begin with the standard(s), objective(s), or essential questions to focus the learning that will take place.

2. Develop the performance or assessment that will demonstrate to what degree each student understands the core ideas or essential question.

3. Determine what experience, activity, or exploration will help students engage with the concept(s) being studied.

4. Create the Explain or sense-making portion of the lesson that would follow the Explore (after sense making occurs, guided practice, problem sets, quizzes, or other resources should be added to solidify learning and deepen proficiency with materials).

5. Design the Engage, if needed, at the beginning of the lesson to motivate student thinking, identify misconceptions, and check prior knowledge.

6. Add Extend opportunities (possibly additional Explore-Explain cycles).

Notice the flow of lesson development is backward in some respects: you start with the objectives being targeted and then move to the final assessment to check mastery before planning the core of the lesson. The creators of Understanding by Design advocated for such an approach many years ago—we have to know our final goal before a meaningful lesson can be assembled (Wiggins & McTighe, 2005).

The Proficient Stage

Teachers in this stage have implemented, through either their own planning or various curricular resources, numerous lessons that focus on inquiry-based instruction. However, they may still face challenges. For instance, students may struggle with adapting to inquiry-based forms of learning; lessons, though engaging, may lack meaning or connection to your goals; or classroom discourse may not sufficiently involve students.

Improve Intentionality

Teachers whose instruction generally aligns with the 4E × 2 Instructional Model (or a similar model) need to focus on the degree or quality of their implementation. Whether used individually, with a peer, or as a department, the EQUIP protocol discussed in Chapter 6 can help assess your strengths and weaknesses among the 19 indicators linked to student achievement. If you have difficulty honestly assessing your practice, it may be helpful to begin by reviewing videos and lesson analyses of other teachers. Free videos and their corresponding EQUIP analyses are available at www.clemson.edu/iim.

Rethink Questioning

Video-recording and then analyzing your instruction is possibly one of the most valuable things that you can do to improve your teaching. After recording, draw a line down the middle of a sheet of paper, play the video, and jot down all the questions that you asked and how you responded to students on the left column. Next, consider how you could have asked better questions or responded to students in a manner that would have improved learning and classroom discourse, and record these ideas in the right-hand column. Especially for small-group work, move from task-oriented questions (e.g., "Are you finished?") to content- or process-focused questions (e.g., "How does running the number of trials that you ran affect the final claims that you can make at the end of the lab?"). If you are stuck regarding what to change, try doing this activity with a peer. Your challenge: aim for meaningful classroom discussion where at least 60 percent of the interaction is student voice.

Reflecting on your questioning is helpful, but being proactive about tomorrow's questions is also vital. On an index card, write three rich, meaningful questions that focus on process or depth of understanding before your next class; then slip the card in your pocket as a reminder of your intentionality. This act of reflection before class takes an area of weakness and begins to transform it into a more natural action: tap into these "pocket" questions as necessary to boost the level of classroom discourse.

Coherence, Coherence, Coherence

Think of your lesson as an amoeba. An amoeba is a fluid, ever-changing organism whose pseudopods continually reshape based on the cytoplasmic fluid streaming inside. Similarly, though your lesson needs to have a solid, coherent structure, it also needs to adapt based on the needs expressed by your students. The coherence of the lesson is based on a logical and consistent relationship among state and national standards, the classroom investigations (explorations), the sense making (explanations), and the assessments. When well executed, the assessments for the lesson actually measure the degree to which the objective was achieved. So if the objective or essential question seeks to have students compare and contrast, then the assessment should be more than multiple-choice questions related to the topic.

The Advanced Stage

At the advanced stage, your inquiry-based instruction is generally successful based on multiple student indicators: deeper interactions, increased efficacy, greater ownership, and improved achievement. At this stage, you continually reflect on what *you* can do to improve the learning in your classroom. When challenges arise—and they will—you do not focus on the ineptness, apathy, or inability of students. Because you understand your students' strengths and weaknesses (through targeted formative and diagnostic assessments), you can devise an approach that will potentially improve student success and learning. Even the best teachers have bad days, but those with advanced skill levels are able to systematically work through issues that may prevent success for students.

Tweaks, Not Overhauls

At the advanced stage, the positives of inquiry-based instruction far outweigh the negatives. To get to this stage, most teachers have been reflective practitioners for quite some time and continue to make intentional changes that improve learning. Changes at this point become specialized and often are situationally dependent. Reviewing EQUIP can provide reminders of targeted areas that need to be improved.

Another continual aspect of instruction is formative assessments that are embedded into the classroom interaction every day. Granted, our society is in an assessment frenzy where assessment fatigue is evident from what often amounts to weeks of standardized district, state, or federal testing during each school year. Testing to satisfy mandates often does little, if anything, to actually improve student learning. Formative assessments, as described earlier, are different in that they should be short, provide immediate feedback to the student and teacher, and help guide the learning that is underway.

Motivating Students

Students were born naturally curious about the world around them. For some, school has stifled that curiosity by focusing on behavior compliance instead. Your goal as an educator is to strike a balance between having a well-managed class and giving students lots of opportunities to ask questions and make sense of their world.

Some may argue that their students are just too apathetic to succeed. Low motivation and student apathy are complex issues. In prior work, I have argued that apathy rears its head via a combination of eight different archetypes (Marshall, 2008). The expressed apathy is usually the result of prior experiences and situations, such as anger, feelings of failure, or boredom from not being challenged. Regardless, apathy exists in various forms in every classroom. The goal is to confront it and find positive ways to move forward.

Just raising your expectations will be enough to reenlist the interest of some students. When students are struggling, it is easy to want to show compassion by lowering your expectations. However, lowering expectations both enables and encourages academic failure. High, reasonable expectations serve many useful purposes; in this case, high expectations are a way of showing students that you have respect for their abilities and are optimistic for their future.

Despite the reason for apathy, building personal meaningful relationships with your students helps reduce apathy and increase motivation. If students know that you truly care about them, they will be more inclined to participate fully in class. At first, this may be to avoid disappointing you. During the year, help them make their motivation more intrinsic so that in the future they will not want to disappoint themselves.

Continually Adapt

The Common Core State Standards in Mathematics and the Next Generation Science Standards remind us all that the foundation of what we study is always evolving. Once you understand how to develop, facilitate, assess, and refine inquiry-based instruction so that learning is maximized, then you are more likely to be able to adapt to the changing landscape of standards, district mandates, or other educational movements. Successful teachers are thoughtful and methodical about what to change, why to change, and how to change so that learning is positively affected. Developing teachers tend to run from or push back on new school, district, state, or national initiatives. While highly successful teachers may also resist some changes, many learn to incorporate that which is valuable for student learning from any initiatives, and they see teaching as a continually evolving endeavor.

TIP Final Thoughts

Part of reflection is to acknowledge where you have grown. What are your greatest strengths relative to inquiry-based instruction? What are two to four ways that you now think differently as a result of reading this book? Finally, what is the one thing that you will do to improve student learning during your next lesson?

Concluding Thoughts

I hope you take away at least the following three main points from this book:

- To maximize learning, students need to be engaged in rich learning opportunities that allow them to explore concepts and ideas *before* they receive formal explanations.

- When you improve the intentionality of your instruction, learning in your classroom also improves.

- A key to transformative teaching is transitioning away from predominantly answer-focused learning to more evidence-focused learning—more why and how and less what.

The 4E × 2 Instructional Model, EQUIP, and the lesson examples presented in this book are strong support mechanisms as you introduce broader and deeper inquiry to your mathematics or science classroom. During the explorations, collaborations, and discourse that characterize inquiry-based instruction, your students will begin to unravel the mysterious and incomprehensible as they weave a fabric of coherent, meaningful, and interconnected knowledge.

TIP Take Away

Reflecting back to the first statement in the introduction, have you been nodding in agreement, saying that you knew all this? Or have you begun to internalize inquiry-based instruction into your practice? Try to summarize the core of inquiry-based practice in 2–3 sentences. Use it as your executive summary (or elevator speech) that you can build from at any time.

I believe that I must be willing to model what I ask of my students and my readers, so my own summary of inquiry-based instruction follows.

Your summary of inquiry learning may differ, and that is perfectly fine. For inquiry-based instruction to be highly effective, there are a few tenets that must occur: (1) students must be able to Explore major concepts before Explanation occurs, (2) teachers must be intentional and purposeful in what they do and why they do it—teaching should be more than just random activities or notes, and (3) students can be pushed toward deeper understanding only when they are actively engaged for significant periods of time.

Appendix: EQUIP

This appendix contains a print copy of the Electronic Quality of Inquiry Protocol (EQUIP) that will allow easy reference as you read the book and reflect on your lessons. EQUIP was devised to help teachers assess their own practice using the 19 indicators and has been used, tested, and refined for more than five years. The protocol provides teachers with a snapshot of how successful a given lesson is in terms of inquiry-based instruction. To underscore what is being measured, here is a reminder of the definition of inquiry-based instruction that we are using:

> **Inquiry-based instruction** is the development of understanding through investigation—that is, asking questions, determining appropriate methods, gathering data, thinking critically about relationships between evidence and explanations, and formulating and communicating logical arguments. (adapted from *National Science Education Standards*, NRC, 1996, p. 105)

You can access EQUIP using these options:

1. Download the free pdf file from www.clemson.edu/iim. Select the research and evaluation tab, then select EQUIP.

2. Download the free app from the App Store. Search for "EQUIP Inquiry Protocol", which will then let you store observations directly on your tablet; or

3. Download the app and link all project data to a personalized database (see www.clemson.edu/iim for instructions).

Registration is free and only takes a few minutes. Registering allows you to access your own records, not simply blank forms.

19 Performance Indicators for Electronic Quality of Inquiry Protocol (EQUIP)

VI. Instructional Factors

Construct Measured	Pre-Inquiry (Level 1)	Developing Inquiry (2)	Proficient Inquiry (3)	Exemplary Inquiry (4)
I1. Instructional Strategies	Teacher predominantly lectured to cover content.	Teacher frequently lectured or used demonstrations to explain content. Activities were verification only.	Teacher occasionally lectured, but students were engaged in activities that helped develop conceptual understanding.	Teacher occasionally lectured, but students were engaged in investigations that promoted strong conceptual understanding.
I2. Order of Instruction	Teacher explained concepts. Students either did not explore concepts or did so only after explanation.	Teacher asked students to explore concept before receiving explanation. Teacher explained.	Teacher asked students to explore before explanation. Teacher and students explained.	Teacher asked students to explore concept before explanation occurred. Though perhaps prompted by the teacher, students provided the explanation.
I3. Teacher Role	Teacher was center of lesson; rarely acted as facilitator.	Teacher was center of lesson; occasionally acted as facilitator.	Teacher frequently acted as facilitator.	Teacher consistently and effectively acted as a facilitator.
I4. Student Role	Students were consistently passive as learners (taking notes, practicing on their own).	Students were active to a small extent as learners (highly engaged for very brief moments or to a small extent throughout lesson).	Students were active as learners (involved in discussions, investigations, or activities, but not consistently and clearly focused).	Students were consistently and effectively active as learners (highly engaged at multiple points during lesson and clearly focused on the task).
I5. Knowledge Acquisition	Student learning focused solely on mastery of facts, information, or rote processes.	Student learning focused on mastery of facts and process skills without much focus on understanding of content.	Student learning required application of concepts and process skills in new situations.	Student learning required depth of understanding to be demonstrated relating to content and process skills.

VII. Discourse Factors

Construct Measured	Pre-Inquiry (Level 1)	Developing Inquiry (2)	Proficient Inquiry (3)	Exemplary Inquiry (4)
D1. Questioning Level	Questioning rarely challenged students above the remembering level.	Questioning rarely challenged students above the understanding level.	Questioning challenged students up to application or analysis levels.	Questioning challenged students at various levels, including at the analysis level or higher; level was varied to scaffold learning.
D2. Complexity of Questions	Questions focused on one correct answer; typically short answer responses.	Questions focused mostly on one correct answer; some open response opportunities.	Questions challenged students to explain, reason, or justify.	Questions required students to explain, reason, or justify. Students were expected to critique others' responses.
D3. Questioning Ecology	Teacher lectured or engaged students in oral questioning that did not lead to discussion.	Teacher occasionally attempted to engage students in discussions or investigations but was not successful.	Teacher successfully engaged students in open-ended questions, discussions, and investigations.	Teacher consistently and effectively engaged students in open-ended questions, discussions, investigations, and reflections.
D4. Communication Pattern	Communication was controlled and directed by teacher and followed a didactic pattern.	Communication was typically controlled and directed by teacher with occasional input from other students; mostly didactic pattern.	Communication was often conversational with some student questions guiding the discussion.	Communication was consistently conversational with student questions often guiding the discussion.
D5. Classroom Interactions	Teacher accepted answers, correcting when necessary, but rarely followed up with further probing.	Teacher or another student occasionally followed up student response with further low-level probe.	Teacher or another student often followed up response with engaging probe that required student to justify reasoning or evidence.	Teacher consistently and effectively facilitated rich classroom dialogue where evidence, assumptions, and reasoning were challenged by teacher or other students.

VIII. Assessment Factors

	Construct Measured	Pre-Inquiry (Level 1)	Developing Inquiry (2)	Proficient Inquiry (3)	Exemplary Inquiry (4)
A1.	Prior Knowledge	Teacher did not assess student prior knowledge.	Teacher assessed student prior knowledge but did not modify instruction based on this knowledge.	Teacher assessed student prior knowledge and then partially modified instruction based on this knowledge.	Teacher assessed student prior knowledge and then modified instruction based on this knowledge.
A2.	Conceptual Development	Teacher encouraged learning by memorization and repetition.	Teacher encouraged product- or answer-focused learning activities that lacked critical thinking.	Teacher encouraged process-focused learning activities that required critical thinking.	Teacher encouraged process-focused learning activities that involved critical thinking that connected learning with other concepts.
A3.	Student Reflection	Teacher did not explicitly encourage students to reflect on their own learning.	Teacher explicitly encouraged students to reflect on their learning but only at a minimal knowledge level.	Teacher explicitly encouraged students to reflect on their learning at an understanding level.	Teacher consistently encouraged students to reflect on their learning at multiple times throughout the lesson; encouraged students to think at higher levels.
A4.	Assessment Type	Formal and informal assessments measured only factual, discrete knowledge.	Formal and informal assessments measured mostly factual, discrete knowledge.	Formal and informal assessments used both factual, discrete knowledge and authentic measures.	Formal and informal assessment methods consistently and effectively used authentic measures.
A5.	Role of Assessing	Teacher solicited predetermined answers from students requiring little explanation or justification.	Teacher solicited information from students to assess understanding.	Teacher solicited explanations from students to assess understanding and then adjusted instruction accordingly.	Teacher frequently and effectively assessed student understanding and adjusted instruction accordingly; challenged evidence and claims made; encouraged curiosity and openness.

IX. Curriculum Factors

Construct Measured	Pre-Inquiry (Level 1)	Developing Inquiry (2)	Proficient Inquiry (3)	Exemplary Inquiry (4)
C1. Content Depth	Lesson provided only superficial coverage of content.	Lesson provided some depth of content but with no connections made to the big picture.	Lesson provided depth of content with some significant connection to the big picture.	Lesson provided depth of content with significant, clear, and explicit connections made to the big picture.
C2. Learner Centrality	Lesson did not engage learner in activities or investigations.	Lesson provided prescribed activities with anticipated results.	Lesson allowed for some flexibility during investigation for student-designed exploration.	Lesson provided flexibility for students to design and carry out their own investigations.
C3. Integration of Content and Investigation	Lesson either content focused or activity focused but not both.	Lesson provided poor integration of content with activity or investigation.	Lesson incorporated student investigation that linked well with content.	Lesson seamlessly integrated the content and the student investigation.
C4. Organizing and Recording Information	Students organized and recorded information in prescriptive ways.	Students had only minor input as to how to organize and record information.	Students regularly organized and recorded information in nonprescriptive ways.	Students organized and recorded information in nonprescriptive ways that allowed them to effectively communicate their learning.

Source: ©2009 Inquiry in Motion, Clemson University, reprinted with permission. Retrieved from Clemson University's Inquiry in Motion Institute, www.clemson.edu/iim; click on Research and Evaluation, then select EQUIP from the menu on the left. The EQUIP interactive web tool is available free from the Apple Store. Search on EQUIP. It is also described as EQUIP (Electronic Quality of Inquiry Protocol), Clemson University.

References

Achieve. (2013). *Next Generation Science Standards*. Retrieved from http://www.nextgen-science.org/

American Association for the Advancement of Science. (1998). *Blueprints for reform*. New York: Oxford University Press.

Atkin, J., & Karplus, R. (1962). Discovery of invention? *Science Teacher, 29*(5), 45.

Barmby, P. (2006). Improving teacher recruitment and retention: The importance of workload and pupil behaviour. *Educational Research, 48*(3), 247–265.

Black, P., Harrison, C., Lee, C., Marshall, B., & Wiliam, D. (2004). Working inside the black box: Assessment for learning in the classroom. *Phi Delta Kappan, 86*(1), 9–21.

Black, P., & Wiliam, D. (1998). Assessment and classroom learning. *Assessment in Education, 5*(1), 7–74.

Blanchard, M. R., Southerland, S. A., Osborne, J., Sampson, V., Annetta, L. A., & Granger, E. (2010). Is inquiry possible in light of accountability? A quantitative comparison of the relative effectiveness of guided inquiry and verification laboratory instruction. *Science Education, 94*(4), 577–616.

Bransford, J. D., Brown, A. L., & Cocking, R. R. (2000). *How people learn: Brain, mind, experience, and school* (Expanded ed.). Washington, DC: National Academies Press.

Bybee, R. W., Taylor, J. A., Gardner, A., Scotter, P. V., Powell, J. C., Westbrook, A., & Landes, N. (2006). *The BSCS 5E Instructional Model: Origins, effectiveness, and applications*. Colorado Springs, CO: Biological Sciences Curriculum Study.

Carin, A. A., Bass, J. E., & Contant, T. L. (2005). *Methods for teaching science as inquiry* (9th ed.). Upper Saddle River, NJ: Pearson.

Costa, A., & Kallick, B. (2000). *Discovering and exploring habits of mind*. Alexandria, VA: ASCD.

Cruickshank, D. R., Jenkins, D. B., & Metcalf, K. K. (2006). *The act of teaching* (4th ed.). New York: McGraw-Hill.

Darling-Hammond, L. (2000). Teacher quality and student achievement: A review of state policy evidence. *Journal of Education Policy Analysis, 8*(1).

Dewey, J. (1910). *How we think*. Lexington, MA: Heath.

Dewey, J. (1938). *Experience and education.* New York: Collier Books.

Donovan, M. S., & Bransford, J. D. (2005). *How students learn: history, mathematics, and science in the classroom.* Washington, DC: National Academies Press.

Dreikers, R., Pepper, F., & Grunwald, B. (1998). *Maintaining sanity in the classroom: Classroom management techniques* (2nd ed.). Florence, KY: Taylor Francis.

Furtak, E. M., Seidel, T., Iverson, H., & Briggs, D. C. (2012). Experimental and quasi-experimental studies of inquiry-based science teaching: A meta-analysis. *Review of Educational Research, 82*(3), 300–329.

Grandmount, R. P. (2003). Judicious discipline: A constitutional approach for public high schools. *American Secondary Education, 31*(3), 97–117.

Hestenes, D., Wells, M., & Swackhamer, G. (1992). Force concept inventory. *The Physics Teacher, 30,* 141–158.

Hudson, S. B., McMahon, K. C., & Overstreet, C. M. (2002). *The 2000 National Survey of Science and Mathematics Education: Compendium of Tables.* Chapel Hill, NC: Horizon Research.

Keeley, P., Eberle, F., & Farrin, L. (2005). *Uncovering student ideas in science: 25 formative assessment probes.* Arlington, VA: National Science Teachers Association Press.

Kohn, A. (1993). *Punished by rewards: The trouble with gold stars, incentive plans, A's, praise, and other bribes.* Boston: Houghton Mifflin.

Llewellyn, D. (2002). *Inquiry within: Implementing inquiry-based science standards.* Thousand Oaks, CA: Corwin Press.

Lotan, R. A. (2006). Managing groupwork in the heterogeneous classroom. In C. M. Evertson & C. S. Weinstein (Eds.), *Handbook of classroom management: Research, practice, and contemporary issues.* Mahwah, NJ: Erlbaum.

Lyman, F. T. (1981). The responsive classroom discussion: The inclusion of all students. In A. S. Anderson (Ed.), *Mainstreaming digest* (pp. 109–113). College Park: University of Maryland Press.

Marshall, J. (2004). Racing with the sun—Inquiry approach to teaching physics. *The Science Teacher, 71*(1), 40–43.

Marshall, J. (2006). Building knowledge and intrigue. *Science Scope, 30*(2), 34–39.

Marshall, J. C. (2007). *4E × 2 Instructional Model.* Retrieved from http://www.clemson.edu/iim

Marshall, J. C. (2008). *Overcoming student apathy: Motivating students for academic success.* Lanham, MD: Rowman & Littlefield.

Marshall, J. C. (2012). *CAREER: Creating effective, sustainable inquiry-based instruction in middle school science classrooms* (DRL-0952160). Clemson, SC: National Science Foundation.

Marshall, J. C., & Horton, R. M. (2011). The relationship of teacher-facilitated inquiry-based instruction to student higher-order thinking. *School Science and Mathematics, 111*(3), 93–101.

Marshall, J. C., Horton, B., & Edmondson, E. (2007). *4E × 2 Instructional Model.* Retrieved from http://www.clemson.edu/iim

Marshall, J. C., Horton, R. M., & Padilla, M. J. (2012). *Center of Excellence for Inquiry in Mathematics and Science.* Columbia, SC: Commission on Higher Education.

Marshall, J. C., Horton, B., & Smart, J. (2009). 4E × 2 Instructional Model: Uniting three learning constructs to improve praxis in science and mathematics classrooms. *Journal of Science Teacher Education, 20*(6), 501–516.

Marshall, J. C., Horton, B., & White, C. (2009). EQUIPping teachers: A protocol to guide and improve inquiry-based instruction. *The Science Teacher, 76*(4), 46–53.

Marshall, J. C., Smart, J., & Horton, R. M. (2010). The design and validation of EQUIP: An instrument to assess inquiry-based instruction. *International Journal of Science and Mathematics Education, 8*(2), 299–321.

Marzano, R. J. (2006). *Classroom assessment and grading that work.* Alexandria, VA: ASCD.

Mergendoller, J. R., Markham, T., Ravitz, J., & Larmer, J. (2006). Pervasive management of project based learning: Teachers as guides and facilitators. In C. M. Evertson & C. S. Weinstein (Eds.), *Handbook of classroom management: Research, practice, and contemporary issues* (pp. 583–614). Mahwah, NJ: Erlbaum.

Minner, D. D., Levy, A. J., & Century, J. (2009). Inquiry-based science instruction—What is it and does it matter? Results from a research synthesis years 1984 to 2002. *Journal of Research in Science Teaching, 47*(4), 1–24.

National Board for Professional Teaching Standards. (1994). *What teachers should know and be able to do.* Washington, DC: Author

National Board for Professional Teaching Standards. (2000). *A distinction that matters: Why national teacher certification makes a difference.* Greensboro, NC: Center for Educational Research and Evaluation.

National Board for Professional Teaching Standards. (2006). *Making a difference in quality teaching and student achievement.* Retrieved October 23, 2006, from http://www.nbpts.org/resources/research

National Council of Teachers of Mathematics. (1998). *Technology conference: NCTM Standards 2000.* Arlington, VA: Author.

National Council of Teachers of Mathematics. (2000). *Principles and standards for school mathematics.* Reston, VA: Author.

National Governors Association Center for Best Practices & Council of Chief State School Officers (NGA Center & CCSSO). (2010). *Common Core State Standards for Mathematics.* Washington, DC: Authors.

National Research Council. (1996). *National science education standards.* Washington, DC: National Academies Press.

National Research Council. (2000). *Inquiry and the national science education standards: A guide for teaching and learning.* Washington, DC: National Academies Press.

National Research Council. (2001). *Adding it up: Helping children learn mathematics.* Washington, DC: National Academies Press.

National Research Council. (2012). *A framework for K–12 science education: Practices, crosscutting concepts, and core ideas.* Washington, DC: National Academies Press.

Partnership for 21st Century Skills. (2013). *Framework for 21st century learners.* Retrieved April 14, 2013, from http://www.p21.org/overview.

Rice, J. K. (2003). *Teacher quality: Understanding the effectiveness of teacher attributes.* Washington, DC: Economic Policy Institute.

Rowe, M. (1987). Wait time: Slowing down may be a way of speeding up. *American Educator, 11*(1), 38–43, 47.

Shepardson, D. P., & Britsch, S. J. (2001). The role of children's journals in elementary school science activities. *Journal of Research in Science Teaching, 38*(1), 43–69.

Stiggins, R. (2005). From formative assessment to assessment FOR learning: A path to success in standards-based schools. *Phi Delta Kappan, 87*(4), 324–328.

Tobias, S., & Everson, H. (2000). Assessing metacognitive knowledge monitoring. In G. Schraw & J. Impara (Eds.), *Issues in the measurement of metacognition* pp. 147–222. Lincoln: Buros Institute, University of Nebraska.

Tobin, K. (1987). The role of wait time in higher cognitive learning. *Review of Educational Research, 56,* 69–95.

Tomlinson, C. A. (2003). *Fulfilling the promise of the differentiated classroom: Strategies and tools for responsive teaching.* Alexandria, VA: ASCD.

van Zee, E. H., Iwasyk, M., Kurose, A., Simpson, D., & Wild, J. (2001). Student and teacher questioning during conversations about science. *Journal of Research in Science Teaching, 38*(2), 159–190.

White, R. T., & Gunstone, R. F. (1992). *Probing understanding.* London: Falmer Press.

Wiggins, G., & McTighe, J. (2005). *Understanding by Design* (Expanded 2nd ed.). Alexandria, VA: ASCD.

Willis, J. (2006). *Research-based strategies to ignite student learning: Insights from a neurologist and classroom teacher.* Alexandria, VA: ASCD.

Wilson, C. D., Taylor, J. A., Kowalski, S. M., & Carlson, J. (2009). The relative effects of equity of inquiry-based and commonplace science teaching on students' knowledge, reasoning, and argumentation. *Journal of Research in Science Teaching, 47*(3), 276–301.

Wilson, J., & Clarke, D. (2004). Towards the modelling of mathematical metacognition. *Mathematics Education Research Journal, 16*(2), 25–48.

Windschitl, M. (2003). Inquiry projects in science teacher education: What can investigative experiences reveal about teacher thinking and eventual classroom practice? *Science Education, 87*(1), 112–143.

Index

Note: The letter *f* following a page number indicates a figure.

About the Author

Jeff C. Marshall is an associate professor in Science Education at Clemson University and is the director of the Inquiry in Motion Institute with the mission of facilitating teacher transformation in K–12 mathematics and science classrooms through rigorous and authentic inquiry-based learning experiences.

A recipient of the Presidential Award for Excellence in Mathematics and Science Teaching, Marshall has published 2 books and more than 40 articles and given more than 80 presentations in the last decade. He consults with school districts, universities, and grant projects, including numerous Improving Teacher Quality grants across the United States. The EQUIP instrument discussed in this book is used by the entire Teacher Quality program in Texas and several other projects to measure the degree of teacher effectiveness relative to inquiry-based instruction.

Marshall earned a bachelor's degree from the University of Central Oklahoma and earned a master's degree and doctorate in curriculum and instruction (with a physics/chemistry emphasis) from Indiana University. He can be contacted at 404-A Tillman Hall, Clemson, SC 29634. Phone: 864-656-2059. E-mail: marsha9@clemson.edu.

Related ASCD Resources: Inquiry Learning, Science, and Math

At the time of publication, the following ASCD resources were available (ASCD stock numbers appear in parentheses). For up-to-date information about ASCD resources, go to www.ascd.org.

ASCD EDge Group

Exchange ideas and connect with other educators interested in student-based inquiry learning, middle school science, and high school mathematics on the social networking site ASCD EDge™ at http://ascdedge.ascd.org/

Print Products

Common Core Standards for Elementary Grades 3–5 Math & English Language Arts: A Quick-Start Guide Amber Evenson, Monette McIver, Susan Ryan, Amitra Schwols and John Kendall (#113015)

Common Core Standards for High School Mathematics: A Quick-Start Guide Amitra Schwols, Kathleen Dempsey and John Kendall (#113011)

Common Core Standards for Middle School Mathematics: A Quick-Start Guide Amitra Schwols, Kathleen Dempsey and John Kendall (#113013)

Concept-Rich Mathematics Instruction: Building a Strong Foundation for Reasoning and Problem Solving Meir Ben-Hur (#106008)

Developing Minds: A Resource Book for Teaching Thinking, 3rd Edition edited by Arthur L. Costa (#101063)

Developing More Curious Minds John Barell (#101246)

How to Assess Higher-Order Thinking Skills in Your Classroom Susan M. Brookhart (#109111)

Inference: Teaching Students to Develop Hypotheses, Evaluate Evidence, and Draw Logical Conclusions // A Strategic Teacher PLC Guide by Harvey F. Silver, R. Thomas Dewing and Matthew J. Perini (#112027)

Learning to Love Math: Teaching Strategies That Change Student Attitudes and Get Results Judy Willis (#108073)

Priorities in Practice: The Essentials of Mathematics, Grades K–6: Effective Curriculum, Instruction, and Assessment Kathy Checkley (#106129)

Priorities in Practice: The Essentials of Mathematics, Grades 7–12: Effective Curriculum, Instruction, and Assessment Kathy Checkley (#106012)

Priorities in Practice: The Essentials of Science, Grades K–6: Effective Curriculum, Instruction, and Assessment Rick Allen (#106206)

Priorities in Practice: The Essentials of Sciences, Grades 7-12, Effective Curriculum, Instruction, and Assessment Rick Allen (#3107119)

Problems as Possibilities: Problem-Based Learning for K-16 Education 2nd ed. Linda Torp and Sara Sage (#101064)

Productive Group Work: How to Engage Students, Build Teamwork, and Promote Understanding Nancy Frey, Douglas Fisher, and Sandi Everlove (#109018)

Total Participation Techniques: Making Every Student an Active Learner Pérsida Himmele & William Himmele (#111037)

THE WHOLE CHILD The Whole Child Initiative helps schools and communities create learning environments that allow students to be healthy, safe, engaged, supported, and challenged. To learn more about other books and resources that relate to the whole child, visit www.wholechildeducation.org.

For more information: send e-mail to member@ascd.org; call 1-800-933-2723 or 703-578-9600, press 2; send a fax to 703-575-5400; or write to Information Services, ASCD, 1703 N. Beauregard St., Alexandria, VA 22311-1714 USA.